quick & easy
low-fat cooking
IN COLOUR

catherine atkinson

foulsham
LONDON • NEW YORK • TORONTO • SYDNEY

foulsham

The Publishing House, Bennetts Close, Cippenham, Slough, Berkshire, SL1 5AP, England

Foulsham books can be found in all good bookshops and direct from www.foulsham.com

ISBN: 978-0-572-03455-9

A CIP record for this book is available from the British Library

Printed in Dubai

Contents

Introduction   4

Eating well to stay well   5

Planning a low-fat diet   7

Easy ways to cut down on fat and saturated fat   9

Weekly meal plans   12

Notes on the recipes   17

Low-fat sweet treats   18

Snacks & light meals   20

Chicken & turkey   40

Beef, pork & lamb   60

Fish & seafood   86

Vegetables & vegetarian   106

Index   126

Introduction

So much has been written about what we should and shouldn't eat that it's hardly surprising if we're sceptical about dietary advice. Conflicting opinions, complicated explanations and confusing terms can make it difficult to separate fact from fiction and you may end up feeling that all the foods you enjoy are 'bad for you'. However, when it comes to avoiding health problems such as heart disease and excess weight, the recommendations are loud and clear; reducing your intake of fat (especially saturated fat) is one of the most important dietary changes you can make to improve your health.

You may have been advised by your doctor or dietician to reduce your fat intake, or have simply resolved to follow a low-fat diet. Either way, a glance through the inspiring recipes in this book will persuade you that it will be a change for the better in every respect.

It's easy to follow a healthy eating plan without becoming faddist – and cutting down on fat needn't mean sacrificing taste. There's no need to go without all your favourite foods, but you may need to choose ingredients that are naturally lower in fat and prepare them with little – if any – additional fat.

This book contains no quick fixes or fads, but it does provide easy-to-follow advice on how to reduce the amount of fat in your diet, plus recipes to suit all tastes and ages. You can still enjoy hearty main courses and desserts that are so delicious it's hard to believe they're good for you, and it won't be long before you develop a preference for low-fat versions of everyday foods.

Most of the recipes can be prepared and cooked within 30 minutes; others need a short preparation time, and are then popped in the oven and left to cook without fuss. With over fifty dishes to choose from, you can eat well and wisely without denying yourself the foods you love. Simply use the Weekly Meal Plans (see pages 12–16) to get you started and you'll never look back.

Eating well to stay well

The links between diet and health are well recognised and there's no doubt that eating a sensible diet can make you look and feel great. Nutritionists constantly talk about the importance of a 'balanced' diet – but it isn't always easy to understand exactly what this means. Current guidelines state that we should all eat more starchy foods, more fruit and vegetables and less fat, sugary and salty food, but our busy lifestyles and fast-food culture make it only too easy to neglect our diet. Reducing your fat intake is probably the most important change you can make to your diet. Extra fruit, vegetables and starchy carbohydrates will help fill the gap, which will not only make your diet healthier but you should also gradually lose weight, should you need to do this.

Fat facts

You do need *some* fat in a healthy balanced diet! We tend to think that all fat is unhealthy, but some types are needed to keep the body healthy by providing fat-soluble vitamins A, D, E and K and the essential fatty acids omega-3 and omega-6 needed for the development and function of the brain, eyes and nervous system. It's not enough simply to know which foods are high in fat and which are low in fat; we also need to understand that there are different kinds of fats and that some of these should be avoided.

The three types of fats are saturated, monounsaturated and polyunsaturated; almost all foods that contain fat have a mixture of all three.

■ SATURATED FATS

These are mainly found in foods of animal origin – meat and dairy products such as butter and lard (shortening), cream and the fat in meat. Saturated fats are known to increase the risk of cardiovascular disease and because of their damaging effects on health you should aim to limit them as much as possible. Try to cut down on 'visible' saturated fat sources, such as butter on bread and the fat on meat such as bacon, as well as 'hidden' fats in cakes, biscuits (cookies) and pastries.

■ MONOUNSATURATED FATS

These are found in foods such as olive oil, some nuts, oily fish and avocado pears. Studies have shown that monounsaturated fat reduces the levels of 'bad' low-density lipoprotein (LDL), which helps lower the level of blood cholesterol. Our bodies can make both saturated and monosaturated fatty acids, so we do not have to eat them.

■ POLYUNSATURATED FATS

These are the ones we need to include in our diet, which is why they are known as 'essential fatty acids'. There are two types: omega-6, which can be found in sunflower, sesame, walnut and wheatgerm oils and seeds; and omega-3, from soya and rapeseed oils, walnuts and oily fish such as salmon. These fats are involved in regulating blood pressure and the immune response.

How much fat?

Fat intake should be no more than 30–35 per cent of total calories each day and saturated fat should be less than 10 per cent of your total calorific intake. The current recommendations from the UK Department of Health are an absolute maximum of 71 g of fat for women each day and 93.5 g for men. Ideally the daily total should be much lower as we require only a small amount of fat each day – just 25 g – to keep us healthy.

Here's how easy it is to eat more than you need:

- butter or margarine on two slices of bread: 16 g fat
- a small bag of crisps (potato chips): 10 g fat
- 3 average-sized pork sausages: 12 g fat
- a small bar of chocolate: 14 g fat

The cholesterol factor

Cholesterol is a waxy substance in your blood that is a major component of every cell wall in your body. It's needed for making many essential hormones and vitamin D. Excessive amounts of cholesterol in the blood can cause cardiovascular disease as cholesterol forms fatty deposits in the arteries, which narrows them and is the most common cause of heart attacks and strokes. For some people, an excess of cholesterol in the blood is a hereditary trait; but for most it is caused by a diet high in both overall fat and – especially – in saturated fat.

Planning a low-fat diet

It's relatively easy to cut down on obvious sources of fat such as butter, cream and the visible fat on meats, but you should also watch out for hidden fats in food. We tend to think of cakes and biscuits as 'sweet' foods but usually more calories come from their fat content than from the sugar. At 9 calories per gram (compared to carbohydrates at 4 calories per gram), it is the most calorie-dense nutrient.

Look at labels

Food labels can be confusing and you'll see all kinds of claims – reduced-fat, lean, light, fat-free and so on. Ingredients are listed in order of quantity, so watch out for those with fat near the top. Food labels are a useful source of information, but don't assume that a product labelled as 'lower in fat' is necessarily a healthy choice – it simply means lower in fat than the normal product, which may still make it very high in fat.

'Traffic light' labelling is used on an increasing number of foods and in many supermarkets. They enable you to see at a glance if the product has high, medium or low amounts of fat and saturated fat. Other labelling may include:

- **Fat-free:** less than 0.5 g of fat per serving.
- **Low-fat:** 3 g or less per serving, or 3 g per 100 g for a meal or main dish, and 30 per cent or less of total calories.
- **Reduced-fat:** 25 per cent less fat than food it is being compared to (so if the original food is very high in fat, the 'reduced-fat' product may still be high in fat).
- **Low saturated fat:** 1 g or less and 15 per cent or less of calories from saturated fat.
- **High in polyunsaturates/low in saturates:** contains at least 35 per cent fat of which at least 45 per cent of the fatty acids are polyunsaturated and not more than 25 per cent saturated.
- **Light/lite:** 50 per cent less fat or one-third fewer calories than the regular product.
- **Lean:** less than 10 g of fat, 4.5 g of saturated fat and 95 mg of cholesterol per 100 g of meat, poultry or seafood.
- **Extra-lean:** less than 5 g of fat, 2 g of saturated fat and 95 mg of cholesterol per serving and per 100 g of meat, poultry or seafood.
- **Low cholesterol:** 20 mg or less of cholesterol per serving and 2 g or less saturated fat per serving.
- **Low-calorie:** 40 calories or less per serving.

When reading labels you should avoid products with high amounts of saturated fat and anything that contains 'hydrogenated' or 'trans fats'. These are vegetable oils that have been artificially hardened during the manufacturing process. They are used by many manufacturers because they can increase a food's shelf life and are cheap. Consequently, they appear in many commercially prepared cakes, biscuits (cookies), pastries and some margarine. Hydrogenated fat is considered to be even more harmful than saturated fat.

Your shopping basket

■ MEAT AND FISH

Red meats – lamb, beef and pork – are a great source of nutrients including protein, iron and zinc, but are also high in saturated fat – and even the leanest-looking meat contains around 10 per cent. Eat these no more than two or three times a week. Check the fat content on packs of minced (ground) meat and choose the lowest, or ask the butcher to mince you a piece of lean meat instead. Chicken and turkey are good choices, but always remove the skin, which is high in fat, before eating. Avoid meat products such as sausages (or try the lower-fat ones or good-quality venison sausages), salami, pâtés and pies. Both white and 'oily' fish are lower in fat than most meats so eat them twice a week; eat oily fish at least once a week as it contains 'beneficial' oils.

■ CHEESE

Cheese is astonishingly high in fat and most of it is saturated. Hard cheese, such as Cheddar, is around one-third fat. It is, however, a useful provider of calcium and a great flavouring ingredient in cooking; just make sure you use it sparingly. Choose a strong-flavoured cheese and you'll find less is needed, or try the reduced-fat alternatives to Cheddar and Cheshire if you are a cheese fan (but they are not so good for cooking). Forget cream cheese – it contains over 45 per cent fat; the low-fat soft cheeses or curd cheese are excellent alternatives and contain only around 10 per cent fat.

■ MILK, CREAM AND YOGHURT

Although the fat content of whole milk is only about 3.9 g per 100 g, you may be drinking quite a lot of it in tea and coffee during the day. If you get through a pint daily, you'll be consuming around 20 g of fat. It's worth switching to skimmed milk, which is virtually fat-free. If you find this too drastic, at least change to semi-skimmed. Many skimmed milk powders and coffee creamers have added fat to give them a richer taste, so check labels carefully. Double (heavy) cream contains a massive 48 per cent fat, so cut it out of your diet completely. Greek-style yoghurt makes a good alternative as it has a rich and creamy taste and is useful in cooking, but it still contains about 10 per cent fat, so it should be used sparingly. Low-fat natural yoghurt has less than 2 per cent fat and, if you want a thicker product, strain it through a sieve (strainer) lined with muslin (cheesecloth) over a bowl in the fridge for several hours or overnight; the whey will drip into the bowl, leaving very thick yoghurt behind.

Easy ways to cut down on fat and saturated fat

Here are some helpful tips for cutting down on fat in your diet and for altering the type of fat you use. While each on its own may reduce the fat you eat by only a little, added together they can make a huge difference to your health.

CUT OUT BUTTER

Why? Butter is high in saturated fat.

Try instead: Sunflower or polyunsaturated margarine or low-fat spread. If you really love the flavour of butter and can't live without it, use less of it and spread it on bread and toast a lot more thinly! When eating foods such as soups, cheese and cold meat, serve them with bread without any spread; this is easier if you choose textured breads such as Granary or French stick. When having meals such as beans or scrambled eggs, don't automatically butter the bread; there's really no need. Don't toss vegetables in butter; if you want to add a glossy finish and extra flavour, toss in the tiniest amount of olive oil and a dash of lemon juice.

CUT OUT LARD, SUET AND BLOCK MARGARINE

Why? These are high in saturated and/or hydrogenated fat. Both vegetarian suet and block margarine are made by hydrogenating fat.

Try instead: White vegetable fat or sunflower margarine.

CUT OUT FAST-FOOD TAKEAWAYS

Why? These are usually fried in partially hydrogenated oil.

Try instead: Healthy home-made stir-fries; low-fat Indian dishes made with yoghurt rather than creamy sauces; grilled (broiled) or baked rather than deep-fried fish.

EAT FEWER FATTY MEATS AND HIGH-FAT PROCESSED MEAT PRODUCTS LIKE SAUSAGES, SALAMI AND PIES

Why? As well as being high in fat, you should try to limit your intake of processed foods.

Try instead: Very lean cuts of meat, reduced-fat sausages and meat products. Try lean ham or turkey rashers (slices) instead of bacon, and sliced chicken or turkey instead of pastrami or corned beef. If you're a pastry (paste) fan, filo pastry brushed with the tiniest amount of oil is a good alternative to puff or shortcrust (basic pie crust).

EAT LESS RICH SALAD DRESSING AND MAYONNAISE

Why? A fatty salad dressing will ruin the healthy advantages of a salad.

Try instead: Dressing made from low-fat yoghurt or fromage frais, or use less dressing but make it with a healthier oil such as olive or walnut. Choose lower-fat or 'light' bottled mayonnaise, but remember that they are still high-fat products.

EAT FEWER HIGH-FAT SNACKS

Why? Crisps (potato chips), cakes, biscuits (cookies) and pastries are high in both fat and sugar – you just don't need them except as occasional treats.

Try instead: Dried fruit mixed with just a few nuts, breadsticks, plain popcorn, lower-fat home-made bakes and cakes.

SWITCH TO LOWER-FAT ALTERNATIVES

Why? You can reduce your fat intake simply by switching to lower-fat alternatives. Check out some of the following:

- **0.2 g fat:** 5 ml/1 tsp whole milk
  200 ml/7 fl oz/scant 1 cup skimmed milk
- **1 g fat:** 120 ml/4 fl oz/½ cup low-fat natural yoghurt
  15 ml/1 tbsp Greek-style yoghurt
- **2.5 g fat:** ¼ bacon rasher (slice)
  8 turkey rashers
- **12 g fat:** 15 g/½ oz butter or margarine
  25 g/1 oz low-fat spread
- **15 g fat:** 50 g/2 oz Cheddar cheese
  65 g/2½ oz Edam (Dutch) cheese
  75 g/3 oz Feta cheese
  100 g/4 oz reduced-fat Cheddar cheese
  200 g/7 oz cottage cheese

Low-fat cooking

You should aim to reduce the fat in your diet by choosing healthy ingredients. But it's not just the food you buy; the way you cook it is just as important. There are plenty of ways to produce tasty meals without adding lots of additional fat.

- Cut down the amount of fat or oil you need when frying or stir-frying by using a good-quality, heavy-based, non-stick frying pan.
- Try the 'wet-frying' technique. Cook foods such as chopped onions in a few tablespoonfuls of stock or a mixture of stock and sherry and wine until tender. You can also cook in stock with the addition of just a little oil, which lets the onions start to brown when all the liquid has evaporated.

- Grilling (broiling) food requires little or no extra fat and gives food a flavoursome crisp exterior. Keep it moist by marinating first or basting as you cook with a light dressing, lemon juice or stock. This is ideal for oily fish fillets – cook them skin-side up on a rack close to the heat until almost cooked, then turn them over and briefly cook the other side. The skin will protect the flesh and stop it from drying out (remove it when serving or eating). Grilling is not suitable for tough cuts of meat, as these will become tougher in the intense heat.

- Invest in a griddle pan. Very little oil is required to stop the food sticking and any excess fat from the food drains into the grooves of the pan.

- Microwave or steam food or oven-cook 'en papillote' (in foil or greaseproof (waxed) paper parcels). These are all great ways to cook tender items such as fish fillets and chicken breasts. The moist environment prevents the food drying out, so no oil is necessary.

- Casseroling, stewing and braising can be great ways to tenderise meat and fat can be kept to a minimum. They're not the fastest ways to cook, but once in the oven the dish can be left to its own devices. Make dishes the day before, cool quickly, then chill overnight in the fridge. You can then skim off the fat that has risen to the top before reheating thoroughly. This is not only a great way of reducing fat, but it also allows the flavours to develop and mingle.

- Use a rack when roasting meat to allow the fat to drip through. Instead of constant basting with oil, loosely cover with foil for most of the cooking time, then remove for the last few minutes to allow the meat to brown.

Which oil should you choose?

All spreads and oils contain a combination of saturated, monounsaturated and polyunsaturated fats in different proportions. Avoid those that are highest in saturated fat completely – but remember that whichever one you choose, oil is 100 per cent fat and just one teaspoonful contains a massive 33 calories.

■ MOSTLY SATURATED
- butter
- hard margarine
- suet
- coconut oil

■ MOSTLY MONOUNSATURATED
- olive oil
- rapeseed oil
- grapeseed oil

■ MOSTLY POLYUNSATURATED
- sunflower oil
- safflower oil
- soya oil
- walnut oil

Weekly meal plans

Here you'll find suggestions for low-fat main meals for 4 weeks to get you started and to introduce you to a new way of healthy eating. There are also shopping lists for each week to save you time.

Aim to start the day with a good breakfast – a couple of slices of toast with a scraping of low-fat spread, or cereal with skimmed milk, plus a piece of fresh fruit or a small glass of fruit juice, is ideal and will provide an essential source of energy for the morning ahead and hopefully stop you snacking until midday.

For lunch, take a look at the Snacks & Light Meals chapter (see page 20) or, if you rely on a canteen or snack-bar, choose low-fat options such as baked potatoes with a baked bean or cottage cheese (no butter) filling. Many shops sell pre-packed lower-fat sandwiches. If not, tuna or chicken with salad are good choices, as long as they not oozing with mayonnaise.

Day	Week 1	Week 2
Monday	Lamb kebabs with cucumber and tomato salsa (see page 79)	Open lasagne with roasted vegetables (see page 125)
Tuesday	Warm chicken salad (see page 52)	Chilli-baked plaice with hot onion relish (see page 90)
Wednesday	Tasty tuna fishcakes (see page 101)	Seared beef with herb and horseradish mash (see page 68)
Thursday	Roasted butternut squash with blue cheese and sage (see page 109)	Greek lamb casserole (see page 83)
Friday	Herb frittata with smoked salmon (see page 93)	Seafood paella (see page 89)
Saturday	Chilli and lime spatchcocked poussins (see page 55)	Vegetarian shepherd's pie (see page 110)
Sunday	Mustard roast beef (see page 67)	Moroccan chicken (see page 51)

Day	Week 3	Week 4
Monday	Herby polenta and mushrooms (see page 113)	Venison sausages with red wine gravy (see page 76)
Tuesday	Five-spice trout and stir-fried vegetables (see page 98)	Salmon teriyaki skewers with lemon rice (see page 105)
Wednesday	Caribbean chicken with sweet potatoes (see page 47)	Turkey and tagliatelle sauté (see page 59)
Thursday	Mozzarella meatballs in rich tomato sauce (see page 71)	Nut loaf with tomato sauce (see page 122)
Friday	Potato-topped cod with green herb dressing (see page 94)	Seafood salad (see page 97)
Saturday	Quick chilli beef (see page 63)	Hot and spicy pork (see page 75)
Sunday	Simple lamb hotpot (see page 80)	Kashmiri chicken (see page 43)

Shopping lists

It can be frustrating to start cooking a dish, only to discover that you don't have all the necessary ingredients. This is a list of absolutely everything you'll need to follow the 4-week meal plan.

■ STORECUPBOARD, FRIDGE AND FREEZER

2 x 200 g/7 oz/small cans of tuna (preferably in spring water)
400 g/14 oz/large can of chopped tomatoes with chilli
4 x 400 g/14 oz/large cans of chopped tomatoes
2 x 200 g/7 oz/small cans of chopped tomatoes
400 g/14 oz/large can of chick peas (garbanzos)
400 g/14 oz/large can of lentils
400 g/14 oz/large can of red kidney beans
400 g/14 oz/large can of reduced-fat coconut milk
200 g/7 oz/small can of sweetcorn
Passata (sieved tomatoes)
Olive oil
Sunflower oil
Toasted sesame oil (or use olive or sunflower oil)
Reduced-fat mayonnaise

Cornichons (gherkins)
Salt
Black peppercorns
Dried mixed herbs
Dried oregano
Dried sage (or use dried mixed herbs)
Dried thyme (or use dried mixed herbs)
Ground coriander
Ground cumin
Ground cinnamon
Ground ginger
Ground paprika
Chinese five-spice powder
Dried chilli flakes
Mild chilli powder
Caribbean seasoning (or use home-made, see page 47)
Bay leaves
Nutmeg
Ground turmeric
Saffron strands (or use ground turmeric)
Sun-dried tomato purée (paste)

Reduced-fat pesto
Pumpkin seeds
Sesame seeds
Mixed nuts (or your favourite type)
Cashew nuts
Dijon mustard
Sweet chilli sauce
Thai fish sauce
Oyster sauce
Creamed horseradish
Redcurrant jelly
Black olives
Cider vinegar or white wine vinegar
Rice or sherry vinegar
Clear honey
Dark soy sauce
Light soy sauce (or use dark)
Japanese soy sauce (or use dark soy sauce)
Mirin (or use medium sherry)
Dry sherry

Medium sherry
Dry white wine
Red wine
Plain (all-purpose) flour
Cornflour (cornstarch)
Light brown sugar
Vegetable stock cubes (or fresh vegetable stock in the freezer)
Stock cubes (or keep fresh stock in the freezer): beef, chicken, lamb pork, fish and vegetable (or vegetable can be substituted for any meat stock)
Long-grain white rice
Dried tagliatelle
Dried pappardelle
Rice noodles
Quick-cook polenta
Couscous
Frozen peas
Frozen mixed (bell) peppers
Frozen leaf spinach

■ WEEK 1

Meat and fish
700 g/1½ lb lean lamb
3 skinless, boneless chicken breasts, about 175 g/6 oz each
2 spatchcocked poussins (Cornish hens), each about 750 g/1¾ lb
1 topside of beef joint, about 1 kg/ 2¼ lb
150 g/5 oz thinly sliced smoked salmon

Dairy and eggs
Butter, preferably unsalted (sweet) or sunflower margarine (you'll need 5 ml/ 1 tsp)
20 g/¾ oz Parmesan cheese
75 g/3 oz Emmenthal (Swiss) cheese
100 g/4 oz blue cheese such as Stilton or Gorgonzola
Plain yoghurt (you'll need 150 ml/ ¼ pint/⅔ cup)
Half-fat crème fraîche (you'll need 60 ml/ 4 tbsp) or plain yoghurt
Skimmed milk (you'll need 200 ml/ 7 fl oz/scant 1 cup)
7 eggs

Fruit and vegetables
2 lemons
3 limes

1 orange
½ cucumber
225 g/8 oz plum tomatoes
100 g/4 oz cherry or baby plum tomatoes
4 spring onions (scallions)
2 courgettes (zucchini)
900 g/2 lb potatoes
2 butternut squashes
2 onions (1 of them small)
2 red onions
2 leeks
Garlic (you'll need 4 cloves)
A small piece of fresh root ginger (or use bottled)
2 red chillies (or use chilli powder)
Mixed fresh herbs such as parsley, chives and dill (dill weed)
Fresh coriander (cilantro)
Fresh sage
100 g/4 oz bag of herb salad or baby salad leaves
A mixed baby leaf salad for serving
2 bags of mixed green salad for serving

Bread and other fresh foods
Wholemeal or white bread for crumbs (75 g/3 oz/1½ cups)
8 oval wholemeal or white pitta breads

■ **WEEK 2**

Meat and fish
750 g/1¾ lb thin sirloin or rump steak
450 g/1 lb lamb neck fillet
4 skinless, boneless chicken breasts, about
    175 g/6 oz each
6 plaice fillets
400 g/14 oz bag of mixed cooked seafood

Dairy and eggs
Skimmed milk (you'll need 350 ml/
    12 fl oz/1⅓ cups)
Parmesan cheese (you'll need 25 g/1 oz)
Reduced-fat crème fraîche (you'll need
    75 ml/5 tbsp)
Feta cheese (you'll need 75 g/3 oz)

Fruit and vegetables
2 lemons
1 lime
750 g/1¾ lb potatoes
750 g/1¾ lb mixed root vegetables such as
    carrots, swede (rutabaga) and parsnips
1 aubergine (eggplant)
450 g/1 lb small potatoes

2 courgettes (zucchini)
3 red (bell) peppers
2 yellow peppers
A green vegetable such as cabbage for
    serving
Sugar snap peas for serving
3 onions
1 red onion
1 shallot
A piece of fresh root ginger (or use
    bottled)
2 red chillies (or use bottled chillies or
    dried chilli flakes)
Garlic (you'll need 7 cloves)
Fresh basil leaves
Fresh chives
Fresh coriander (cilantro)
Fresh parsley

Bread and other fresh foods
Fresh lasagne (you'll need 12 sheets)
300 g/11 oz minced (ground) Quorn
Reduced-fat guacamole for serving

■ **WEEK 3**

Meat and fish
8 chicken thighs
350 g/12 oz lean minced (ground) beef
175 g/6 oz lean minced pork
4 boneless lamb leg steaks, about
    500 g/1 lb 2 oz in total
4 trout fillets
4 cod loin fillets, each about 200 g/7 oz

Dairy and eggs
Eggs (you'll need 1)
Emmenthal (Swiss) cheese (you'll need
    50 g/2 oz)
Reduced-fat Mozzarella cheese (you'll
    need 75 g/3 oz)
Sunflower margarine
Low-fat spread (or use sunflower
    margarine) (you'll need 30 ml/2 tbsp)
Skimmed milk (you'll need 15 ml/1 tbsp)
Crème fraîche (you'll need 150 ml/
    ¼ pint/⅔ cup)

Fruit and vegetables
2 lemons (1 to use for the juice, or use
    bottled)
4 onions (1 small, 1 medium and
    2 large)
5 carrots
1 celery stick
Garlic (you'll need 4 cloves)
½ small Savoy cabbage
350 g/12 oz small new potatoes
4 large baking potatoes
450 g/1 lb sweet potatoes
1 red (bell) pepper
225 g/8 oz button mushrooms
225 g/8 oz shiitake mushrooms
450 g/1 lb mixed mushrooms such as
    chestnut, oyster and shiitake
400 g/14 oz fine green beans
Squash for serving
Mangetout (snow peas) for serving
1 bunch of spring onions (scallions)

A piece of fresh root ginger (or use
    bottled)
Fresh chives
Fresh coriander (cilantro)
Fresh parsley
Fresh thyme (or use dried)
Mixed fresh herbs such as parsley, chives,
    tarragon and basil

■ WEEK 4

Meat and fish
8 small squid
12 cooked and peeled tiger prawns
    (shrimp)
8 venison sausages
350 g/12 oz lean minced (ground) pork
350 g/12 oz turkey escalopes
4 skinless, boneless chicken breasts,
    about 175 g/6 oz each
600 g/1 lb 6 oz thick salmon fillets

Dairy and eggs
Mature Cheddar cheese (you'll need 50 g/
    2 oz)
Eggs (you'll need 1)
Thick plain yoghurt (you'll need 300 ml/
    ½ pint/1¼ cups)

Fruit and vegetables
1 lemon
1 orange
2 limes
2 shallots

Bread and other fresh foods
White bread for breadcrumbs (you'll need
    50 g/2 oz/1 cup)
Crusty French bread for serving
Herb-flavoured foccacia or ciabatta for
    serving

2 onions
10 spring onions (scallions)
2 red chillies (or use bottled)
1 leek
A green vegetable such as beans for
    serving
Garlic (you'll need 6 cloves)
150 g/5 oz button mushrooms
225 g/8 oz mushrooms
2 red (bell) peppers
2 large carrots
1 small avocado
100 g/4 oz small ripe tomatoes
50 g/2 oz baby spinach leaves
A piece of fresh root ginger (or use
    bottled)
Fresh mint
Fresh parsley
Fresh sage
Fresh thyme
100 g/4 oz mixed salad leaves

Notes on the recipes

- Do not mix metric, imperial and American measures. Follow one set only.
- American terms are given in brackets.
- The ingredients are listed in the order in which they are used in the recipe.
- Spoon measurements are level: 1 tsp = 5 ml; 1 tbsp = 15 ml.
- Eggs are medium unless otherwise stated.
- Milk is skimmed (but you can use semi-skimmed or soya 'milk').
- Where appropriate, readily available reduced-fat products, such as half-fat crème fraîche and mayonnaise, low-fat yoghurt and reduced-fat cheeses, have been used.
- Always wash, peel, core and seed, if necessary, fresh foods before use. Ensure that all produce is as fresh as possible and in good condition.
- Salt and pepper are included in many recipes, but you should avoid over-seasoning with salt and preferably use a low-sodium version. The use of strongly flavoured ingredients such as garlic and ginger depends on personal taste and quantities can be adjusted accordingly.
- Always use fresh herbs unless dried are specifically called for. If it is necessary to use dried herbs, use a third to half the quantity stated. Chopped frozen varieties are much better than dried. There is no substitute for fresh parsley or coriander (cilantro).
- Can and packet sizes are approximate and will depend on the particular brand.
- Approximate timings are given for making each dish from start to finish and include both preparation and cooking.
- Always preheat a conventional oven and cook on the centre shelf, unless otherwise stated.
- Use whichever kitchen gadgets you like to speed up preparation and cooking times.
- The recipes and advice given in this book are intended as a guide for those wishing to follow a low-fat diet. If you are worried about any aspect of your health, consult your doctor before changing your diet.

Low-fat sweet treats

The sweet dish served at the end of a meal is eagerly anticipated and even when you follow a low-fat diet you don't have to miss out. While fresh fruit and yoghurts are usually an easy and healthy option, many puddings can fit perfectly into a low-fat diet. Here you'll find a selection of delectable reduced-fat desserts suitable for any occasion. Many are lighter versions of popular classics and you may find that no one even notices that these are healthier desserts.

The dessert recipes serve four; the muffin recipe will make six.

Quick and easy desserts

■ FEATHER-LIGHT PEAR PUDDING

Preheat the oven to 180°C/350°F/gas 4/fan oven 160°C. Drain a 400 g/14 oz/large can of sliced pears in natural juice, reserving the juice. Put the pears in a 1 litre/1¾ pint/ 4 cup pie dish with 45 ml/3 tbsp of the juice. Put 50 g/2 oz/4 tbsp of low-fat spread and 40 g/1½ oz/¼ cup of light brown sugar in a bowl. Sift over 100 g/4 oz/1 cup of plain (all-purpose) flour, 5 ml/1 tsp of baking powder and 2.5 ml/½ tsp of ground cinnamon. Lightly beat together 1 egg and 60 ml/4 tbsp of the reserved juice. Add to the bowl and beat for 3–4 minutes until thoroughly mixed. Spoon the sponge mixture over the pears and level the top. Bake for 25–30 minutes or until the sponge is springy to the touch. Dust the top with 10 ml/2 tsp of icing (confectioners') sugar before serving with low-fat custard or 'light' ice-cream.

■ FRESH RASPBERRY BRÛLÉE

Divide 225 g/8 oz of fresh raspberries between four 150 ml/¼ pint/⅔ cup ramekins (custard cups). If liked, drizzle each with a little raspberry or orange liqueur. Blend 100 g/4 oz/1 cup of low-fat soft cheese with 150 ml/¼ pint/⅔ cup of half-fat Greek-style yoghurt and 5 ml/1 tsp of vanilla essence (extract). Spoon the mixture over the raspberries, levelling the tops smooth. Chill in the fridge while making the caramel topping. Put 100 g/4 oz/½ cup of caster (superfine) sugar and 45 ml/3 tbsp of cold water in a heavy-based saucepan. Heat gently, stirring, until the sugar has dissolved. Stop stirring and boil for about 10 minutes or until the mixture turns a rich but not dark golden-brown. Remove from the heat and leave for 3 minutes, then very carefully pour over the cheese mixture. Chill in the fridge until the caramel has set and hardened.

■ HOT SPICED TROPICAL FRUIT KEBABS

Soak four wooden skewers in cold water while preparing the fruit. Quarter 2 large fresh figs, peel 1 large ripe mango and cut the flesh into cubes and drain a 200 g/7 oz/small can of pineapple chunks in natural juice. Thread the fruit on to the skewers and place on a grill (broiler) pan lined with foil. Drizzle with 30 ml/2 tbsp of clear honey and sprinkle with a pinch each of ground ginger and ground cinnamon. Cook under a hot grill (broiler) for about 3 minutes on each side. Serve with a little thick plain yoghurt, if liked.

FLUFFY STRAWBERRY FOOL

Hull and halve 450 g/1 lb of ripe strawberries. Put in a pan with 15 ml/1 tbsp of water and 10 ml/2 tsp of caster (superfine) sugar. Simmer over a low heat for 2 minutes until just soft. Blend 2.5 ml/½ tsp of arrowroot with 15 ml/1 tbsp of cold water. Add to the fruit and simmer for a further minute until thickened. Leave to cool, then spoon about two-thirds of the fruit mixture into four individual glasses and chill in the fridge while making the topping. Purée the rest of the mixture in a blender (you can sieve (strain) it to remove the pips, if preferred). Lightly whip 150 ml/¼ pint/⅔ cup of half-fat whipping cream and 5 ml/1 tsp of vanilla essence (extract) until soft peaks form. Fold in the fruit purée and spoon on top of the fruit mixture in the glasses. Chill until ready to serve.

RICOTTA TIRAMISU

Break 8 boudoir biscuits (sponge fingers) or savoiardi into bite-sized pieces and divide between four glasses. Stir 5 ml/1 tsp of caster (superfine) sugar and 30 ml/2 tbsp of coffee liqueur or brandy into 120 ml/4 fl oz/½ cup of warm espresso coffee and spoon over the sponge fingers. Beat together 200 g/7 oz/scant 1 cup of ricotta cheese, 150 ml/¼ pint/⅔ cup of Greek-style yoghurt, 5 ml/1 tsp of vanilla essence (extract) and 45 ml/3 tbsp of sifted icing (confectioners') sugar. Spoon the mixture over the soaked biscuits. Sprinkle 2.5 ml/½ tsp of good-quality drinking chocolate (sweetened chocolate) powder over each before serving.

SIMPLE CHOCOLATE SOUFFLÉS

Put a baking (cookie) sheet in the oven and preheat to 190°C/375°F/gas mark 5/fan oven 170°C. Roughly chop 50 g/2 oz of plain (semi-sweet) chocolate and put in a non-stick pan with 45 ml/3 tbsp of light brown sugar. Sift over 10 ml/2 tsp of cornflour (cornstarch) and 15 ml/1 tbsp of cocoa (unsweetened chocolate) powder. Add 45 ml/3 tbsp of skimmed milk and blend to a smooth paste, then stir in a further 100 ml/3½ fl oz/scant ½ cup of skimmed milk. Bring to the boil, stirring all the time, until the mixture thickens. Remove from the heat. Separate 2 eggs and stir the yolks into the chocolate mixture. Whisk the whites until stiff and fold half at a time into the mixture. Divide the mixture between four 150 ml/¼ pint/⅔ cup ramekins (custard cups), place on the hot baking sheet and cook for 10–12 minutes until well-risen. Dust with icing (confectioners') sugar and serve at once.

WHOLEMEAL BANANA AND WALNUT MUFFINS

Preheat the oven to 200°C/400°F/gas mark 6/fan oven 180°C. Line a 6-cup muffin tin with paper muffin cases. Mix together 75 g/3 oz/¾ cup of wholemeal flour, 75 g/3 oz/¾ cup of self-raising flour, 15 ml/1 tbsp of light brown sugar and 25 g/1 oz/¼ cup of chopped walnuts in a bowl. Mash 2 really ripe bananas until fairly smooth, then add 20 ml/1½ tbsp of walnut or sunflower oil, 1 beaten egg, 45 ml/3 tbsp of plain yoghurt and 15 ml/1 tbsp clear honey. Add to the dry ingredients and mix briefly until just combined. Divide the mixture between the muffin cases and bake for 20 minutes until well risen and golden-brown. Serve warm or cold.

snacks & light meals

Whether you eat your main meal at midday or in the evening, it's relatively easy to plan and shop for the dish of the day. It's the lunches, suppers and those snacks in between that can be more difficult to cater for. When hunger hits at a time when you're busy and in a hurry, it's only too easy to forget healthy eating and pop out for a pizza or nibble on a few biscuits or a bag of crisps to fill the gap – and before you know it you'll have consumed far more fat than you intended in a not particularly nutritious way.

The recipes in this chapter aim to help solve this problem and you'll find plenty of quick and easy low-fat ideas here. Some, such as Hoisin Turkey Muffins (see page 23) and Roasted Tomato and Rocket Bruschetta (see page 36), can be made in around 15 minutes. Others, such as Leek, Pea and Stilton Soup (see page 27) can be prepared the day before and simply reheated when you're ready to eat.

Hoisin turkey muffins

Serves 4
Ready in 15 minutes

4 white or wholemeal muffins, split
6 spring onions (scallions), trimmed and sliced
15 ml/1 tbsp sesame seeds, preferably toasted
10 ml/2 tsp sesame oil
5 ml/1 tsp fresh or bottled grated root ginger
10 ml/2 tsp water
90 ml/6 tbsp hoisin sauce
350 g/12 oz cooked turkey, shredded
Salt and freshly ground black pepper

1 Preheat the grill (broiler) to medium-hot. Arrange the split muffins, crust-sides up, on the grill pan and cook for 1–2 minutes or until lightly toasted. Turn over and cook the other sides for 30 seconds or until dry but not beginning to brown.

2 Mix the spring onions with 10 ml/2 tsp of the sesame seeds and the oil. Spread this mixture evenly over the muffins, then grill (broil) for 2–3 minutes or until lightly browned.

3 Meanwhile, gently heat the grated ginger and water in a small pan for a few seconds, stirring all the time. Add the hoisin sauce and let the mixture bubble for 30 seconds. Remove the pan from the heat.

4 Pile the turkey on to the spring-onion topped muffins. Spoon the hot hoisin sauce mixture over, sprinkle with the remaining sesame seeds and season with salt and pepper. Serve straight away.

Tips

★ Hoisin sauce is a thick and sticky brown-coloured sauce made from soy beans, garlic, chilli and vinegar. It adds lots of flavour to these muffins.

★ Cooked chicken or lean pork would be a good alternative to the turkey.

Grilled vegetable skewers

 Serves 4
Ready in 25 minutes

8 shallots

2 baby aubergines, trimmed and cut into 2.5 cm/1 in chunks

1 yellow (bell) pepper, de-seeded and cut into 2.5 cm/1 in chunks

100 g/4 oz baby button mushrooms

1 large courgette (zucchini), thickly sliced

100 g/4 oz cherry tomatoes

2 garlic cloves, peeled and thinly sliced

10 ml/2 tsp olive oil

15 ml/1 tbsp balsamic condiment

Salt and freshly ground black pepper

15 ml/1 tbsp chopped fresh parsley (optional)

1 Put the shallots in a heatproof bowl and pour over enough boiling water to cover them. Leave to stand while preparing the rest of the vegetables. If using wooden skewers, put them in cold water to soak (this helps prevent them from charring during cooking).

2 Put the prepared aubergines, pepper, mushrooms, courgette, cherry tomatoes and garlic cloves into a bowl.

3 Drain the shallots and cut off the tops and root ends with a sharp knife. Slip them out of their skins. Add the peeled shallots to the vegetables. Drizzle the oil and balsamic condiment over the vegetables. Lightly season with salt and pepper and gently mix everything together.

4 Line a grill (broiler) pan with foil and preheat the grill to moderately hot. Thread the vegetables on to 8 skewers. Grill for 10 minutes, turning occasionally, until lightly browned and tender. Sprinkle with chopped parsley, if using, before serving.

Serve with: Warmed pitta breads and herb-flavoured rice

Tip

★ For the herb-flavoured rice, cook 225 g/8 oz/1 cup long-grain rice in boiling salted water or stock for 10 minutes. Drain well, then return to the pan and stir in 30 ml/2 tbsp of chopped herbs such as mint or parsley and season with pepper. Spoon into lightly oiled ramekin dishes (custard cups), pressing down gently. Turn out and garnish with a sprig of fresh herbs.

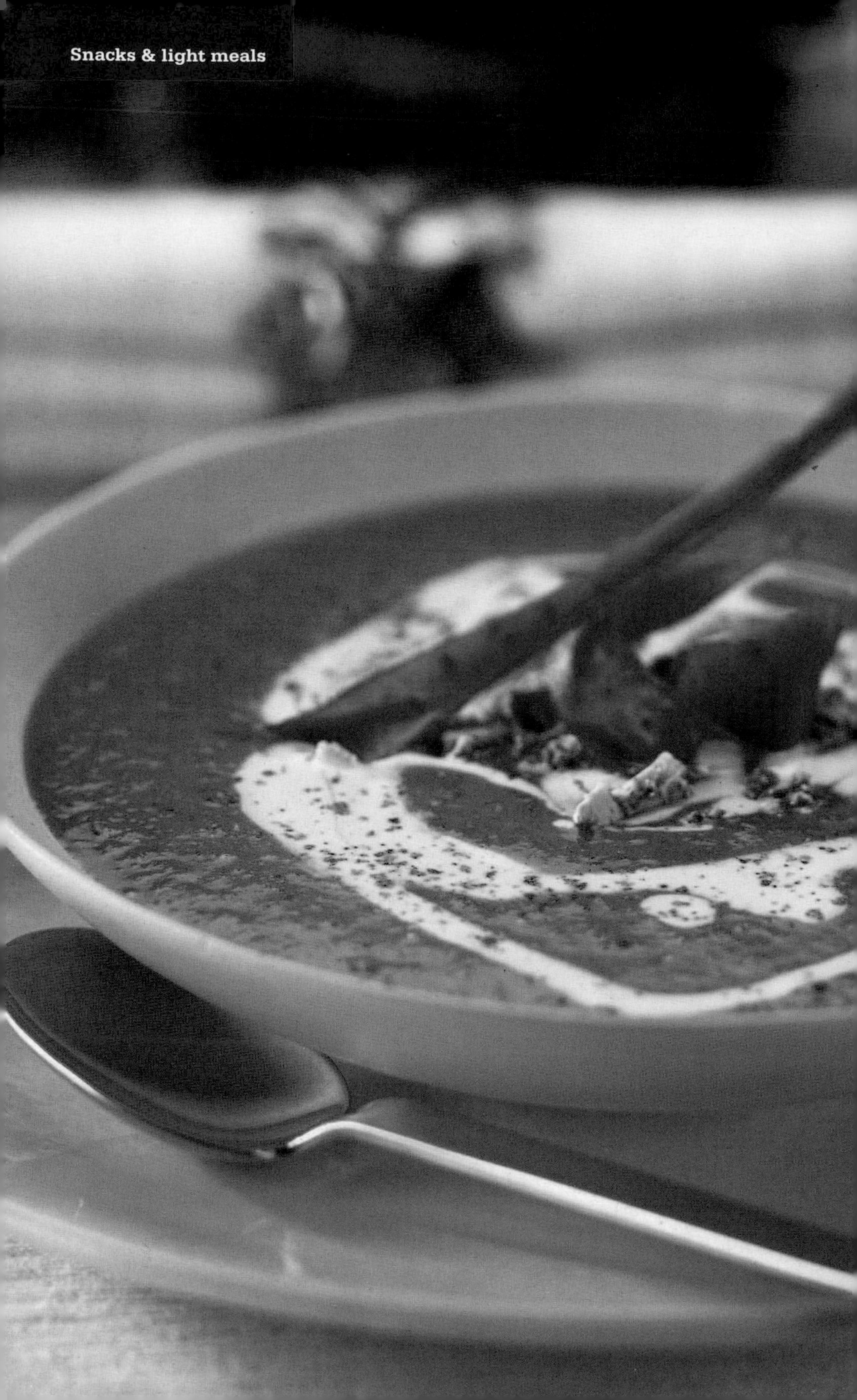

Leek, pea and stilton soup

Serves 4
Ready in 40 minutes

15 g/½ oz/1 tbsp low-fat spread

2 leeks, thinly sliced

750 ml/1¼ pints/3 cups vegetable stock

175 g/6 oz potatoes, peeled and cut into chunks

175 g/6 oz fresh or frozen peas

15 ml/1 tbsp roughly chopped fresh parsley

Salt and freshly ground black pepper

60 ml/4 tbsp low-fat plain yoghurt

40 g/1½ oz Stilton cheese, crumbled

1 Melt the low-fat spread in a small saucepan. Add the leeks and 45 ml/3 tbsp of the stock and cook, stirring, for 2 minutes. Cover the pan with a lid and cook over a low heat for 5 minutes.

2 Stir in the potatoes and the remaining stock. Bring to the boil, then half-cover with the lid and simmer for 15 minutes.

3 Add the peas and parsley and season with salt and pepper, then simmer for a further 3–4 minutes or until all the vegetables are tender. Allow the soup to cool slightly, then purée it in a food processor or blender until smooth.

4 Return the soup to the pan and bring back to the boil. Taste and adjust the seasoning if necessary, then ladle into warm bowls. Serve each portion with a swirl of yoghurt and sprinkling of crumbled Stilton.

Tips

★ This soup is delicious garnished with parsnip crisps. Preheat the oven to 220°C/425°F/gas 7/fan oven 200°C. Peel 2 parsnips and cut into very thin slices using a sharp knife, a mandolin or the fine slicing blade in a food processor. Toss the slices in 10 ml/2 tsp of sunflower oil until they are lightly coated, then spread them out in a single layer on a large non-stick baking (cookie) sheet. Sprinkle evenly with a little salt. Bake for 25 minutes, turning frequently, until crisp and golden, removing any around the edges that are done. Serve a few on top of the soup and the rest separately.

★ To prepare the soup ahead, follow steps 1–3, then pour the soup into a bowl and leave to cool completely. Cover and keep chilled in the fridge for up to 2 days. Alternatively, transfer to a freezerproof container (or freeze in individual portions) and freeze for up to a month; the soup may separate slightly when defrosted, but will be fine when reheated.

Ham and cheese
baked peppers

Serves 4
Ready in 45 minutes

10 ml/2 tsp olive oil

5 ml/1 tsp water

1 large onion, finely chopped

1 large garlic clove, peeled and crushed

6 ripe tomatoes, skinned, seeded and chopped

Salt and freshly ground black pepper

4 medium red or yellow (bell) peppers

100 g/4 oz lean, thickly sliced ham, chopped

75 g/3 oz half-fat Mozzarella cheese, coarsely grated

1 Preheat the oven to 160°C/325°F/gas 3/fan oven 140°C. Heat the oil and water in a frying pan, add the onion and cook gently for 10 minutes until soft. Stir in the garlic and cook for a further minute, stirring all the time.

2 Stir the tomatoes into the onion mixture and season generously with salt and pepper. Turn off the heat.

3 Halve the peppers lengthways through the stems and carefully cut away and discard the white core and seeds. Spoon the tomato mixture into the pepper halves, cover with foil and bake for 30 minutes or until the peppers are tender.

4 Remove the foil and sprinkle the ham on top of the tomato mixture, followed by the Mozzarella. Return to the oven for 5 more minutes or until the cheese has melted. Serve straight away.

Serve with: Crusty white or granary bread

Tip

★ To skin tomatoes, put them in a heatproof bowl and pour over enough boiling water to cover. Leave for 1 minute, then drain and briefly rinse under cold water. The skins should peel away easily.

Roasted vegetable wraps

Serves 4
Ready in 30 minutes

1 red (bell) pepper, seeded and sliced into strips

1 yellow pepper, seeded and sliced into strips

1 red onion, peeled and thickly sliced

2 courgettes (zucchini), cut into 3mm/⅛ in slices

2 large tomatoes, diced

2 garlic cloves, peeled and crushed

15 ml/1 tbsp olive oil

Salt and freshly ground black pepper

30 ml/2 tbsp roughly chopped fresh parsley

4 soft flour tortilla wraps, each about 20 cm/8 in in diameter

150 ml/¼ pint/⅔ cup reduced-fat guacamole or houmous, plus extra to serve garnished with sliced chillies

A few sprigs of parsley to garnish (optional)

1 Preheat the oven to 200°C/400°F/gas 6/fan oven 180°C. Put the pepper strips, onion, courgettes, tomatoes and garlic in a small roasting tin and drizzle with the oil. Season with a little salt and pepper, then toss together until everything is lightly coated with oil.

2 Roast the vegetables for 20–25 minutes, turning once or twice during cooking, until they are very tender and lightly charred. Leave to cool for a few minutes, then sprinkle with the chopped parsley and mix together.

3 About 5 minutes before the end of cooking time, stack the tortillas and wrap them in foil. Put on the oven shelf below the roasting vegetables to warm through.

4 To serve, thinly spread each tortilla with a heaped tablespoonful of guacamole or houmous, leaving a 1 cm/½ in margin around the edge. Spoon a quarter of the roasted vegetables in a pile down the middle, then fold into a cone shape. Serve straight away garnished with sprigs of parsley, if liked, and extra guacamole or houmous.

Tip

★ For a really low-fat spicy pea dip to spread on and to serve with the tortillas, blend together 175 g/6 oz/generous 1 cup of peas, 1 crushed garlic clove, 2 chopped spring onions (scallions), 15 ml/ 1 tbsp of reduced-fat mayonnaise, the juice of ½ lime, a pinch of ground cumin and 30 ml/2 tbsp of roughly chopped fresh coriander (cilantro). Season to taste with salt and pepper and a little more lime juice, if needed.

Prawn noodle salad

Serves 4
Ready in 20 minutes

200 g/7 oz medium egg noodles
1 Little Gem lettuce, thinly sliced
50 g/2 oz button mushrooms, thinly sliced
6 spring onions (scallions), thinly sliced
50 g/2 oz/1 cup beansprouts
400 g/14 oz cooked, peeled tiger prawns (shrimp) or mixed cooked seafood
30 ml/2 tbsp chopped fresh coriander (cilantro)
45 ml/3 tbsp chopped fresh mint
For the dressing:
Juice of 1 lime
15 ml/1 tbsp olive oil
15 ml/1 tbsp light soy sauce
15 ml/1 tbsp water
5 ml/1 tsp fresh or bottled grated root ginger
1 red chilli, seeded and very finely chopped
5 ml/1 tsp caster (superfine) sugar
Freshly ground black pepper
A few fresh herb leaves to garnish (optional)

1 Cook the noodles in plenty of lightly salted boiling water for 3–4 minutes or according to the packet instructions until just tender. Drain and gently rinse under cold water to stop the noodles cooking further. Drain again.

2 Put the noodles in a bowl with the lettuce, mushrooms, spring onions, beansprouts, prawns or seafood and herbs. Gently mix everything together.

3 To make the dressing, whisk together the lime juice, oil, soy sauce, water, ginger, chilli and sugar in a bowl, or shake them in a screw-topped jar. Season to taste with a little pepper (you shouldn't need to add any salt as there is plenty in the soy sauce).

4 Drizzle half the dressing over the salad and gently mix together again. Just before serving, drizzle the remaining dressing over the salad and garnish with a few fresh herb leaves, if liked.

Tip

★ You could cook the noodles in vegetable stock instead of water for added flavour.

Poached eggs and ham
with watercress dressing

Serves 4
Ready in 20 minutes

For the watercress dressing:
75 g/3 oz watercress
150 g/5 oz reduced-fat Greek-style yoghurt
30 ml/2 tbsp reduced-fat mayonnaise
15 ml/1 tbsp lemon juice
A pinch of cayenne pepper
For the eggs and ham:
4 slices of ciabatta or rye bread
8 thin slices of lean cooked ham
Freshly ground black pepper
15 ml/1 tbsp wine vinegar
4 eggs

1 To prepare the watercress dressing, reserve 12 large sprigs of the watercress, then roughly chop the rest and put in a food processor with the yoghurt, mayonnaise, 10 ml/2 tsp of the lemon juice and the cayenne pepper. Blend until the watercress is finely chopped but still has a little texture.

2 Preheat the grill (broiler) and toast the slices of bread on both sides until lightly browned. Place on individual serving plates, then top each slice with 2 slices of ham and 3 sprigs of watercress. Grind over a little black pepper.

3 Pour about 4 cm/1½ in of water into a frying pan. Add the vinegar and bring to the boil, then reduce the heat to keep the water bubbling gently. Crack an egg into a small dish, then gently tip it into the bubbling water. Quickly repeat this with the remaining eggs. Cook each egg very gently for 1 minute undisturbed, then gently spoon a little of the bubbling water over the middle of the egg to cook the yolk.

4 When the eggs are cooked to your liking, use a slotted spoon to carefully lift them out of the water, draining them well. Pat the egg dry with kitchen paper (paper towels), then place on top of the ham. Taste the watercress sauce and add the rest of the lemon juice, if liked. Spoon over the ham and eggs and serve straight away.

Tip

★ If you prefer, use 4 slices of Parma ham (about 50 g/2 oz in total) instead of ham, but make sure you cut away all the fat.

Roasted tomato and rocket
bruschetta

Serves 4
Ready in 15 minutes

700 g/1½ lb cherry tomatoes, preferably on the vine

5 ml/1 tsp olive oil

2.5 ml/½ tsp caster (superfine) sugar

Salt and freshly ground black pepper

1 ciabatta loaf

2 garlic cloves, halved

A handful of rocket leaves

25 g/1 oz Parmesan cheese shavings

1 Preheat the grill (broiler) to high and line the grill pan with foil. Toss the tomatoes with the oil and sugar, then season lightly with salt and pepper. Grill (broil) for 8–10 minutes, turning occasionally, until the tomatoes begin to split and caramelise. Remove from the grill and set aside.

2 Meanwhile, cut the ciabatta into 8 thick slices. Toast under the grill for about 1 minute on each side until golden and crisp, then rub with the cut garlic cloves.

3 Top the ciabatta slices with the rocket, then arrange the cherry tomatoes on top, spooning any juices over. Sprinkle with the Parmesan shavings before serving.

Tips

★ To make grilled pepper and cherry tomato bruschetta, halve and seed 1 red and 1 yellow (bell) pepper. Place the peppers skin-sides up on the grill tray and grill for 8–10 minutes or until the flesh softens and the skin begins to char and blister. Add 175 g/6 oz of halved cherry tomatoes to the grill for the last 2 minutes of cooking. Place the peppers in a polythene bag, twist the top to keep in the steam, then leave until cool enough to handle. Once cold, peel off the skins and roughly chop the flesh. Put in a bowl with the tomatoes and sprinkle with 10 ml/2 tsp of balsamic condiment and salt and freshly ground black pepper to taste. Pile on top of the garlic-flavoured slices of ciabatta.

★ Parmesan is made with semi-skimmed cow's milk and, although it is fairly high in fat, it has a strong, savoury flavour so only a little is needed for this recipe.

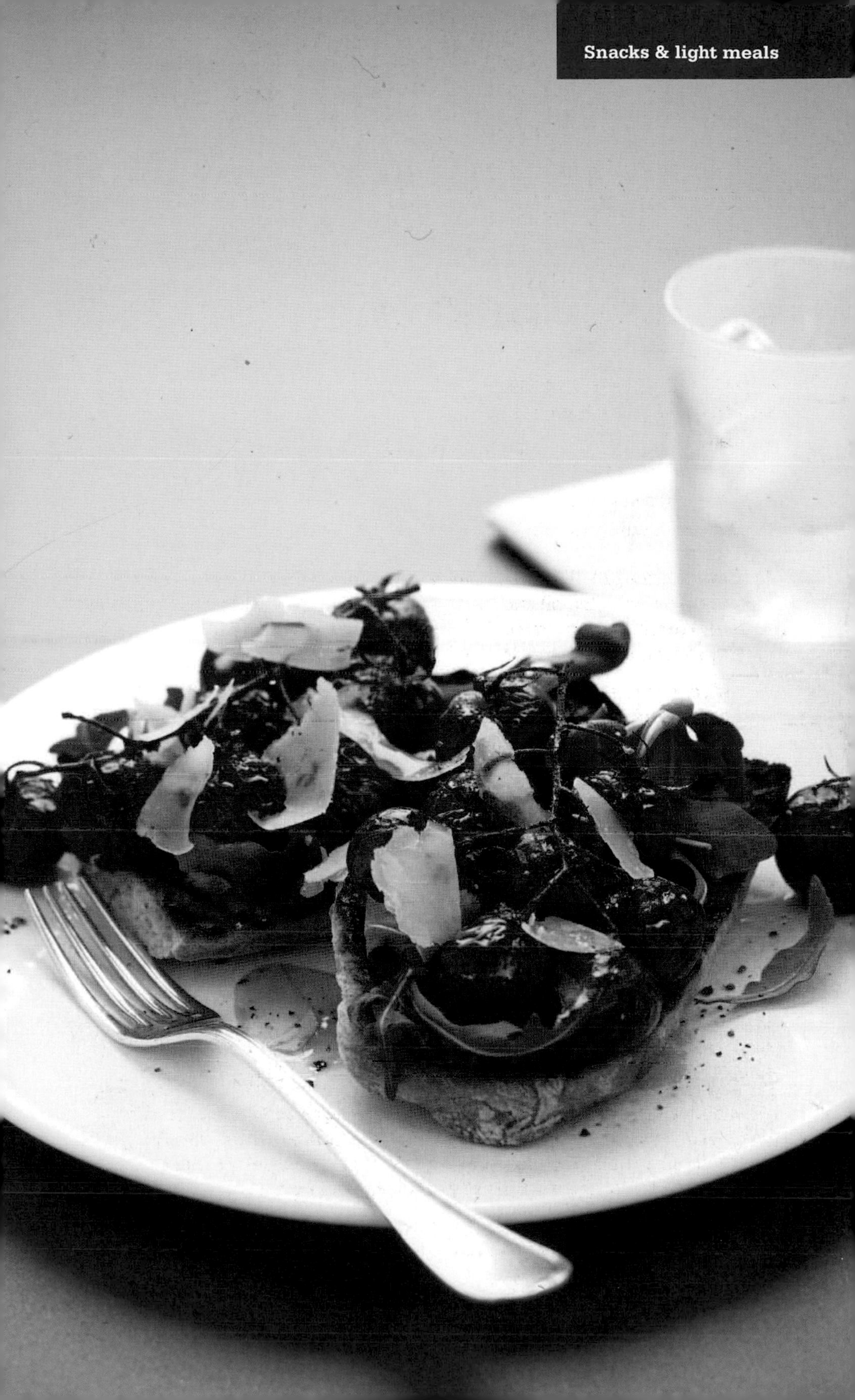

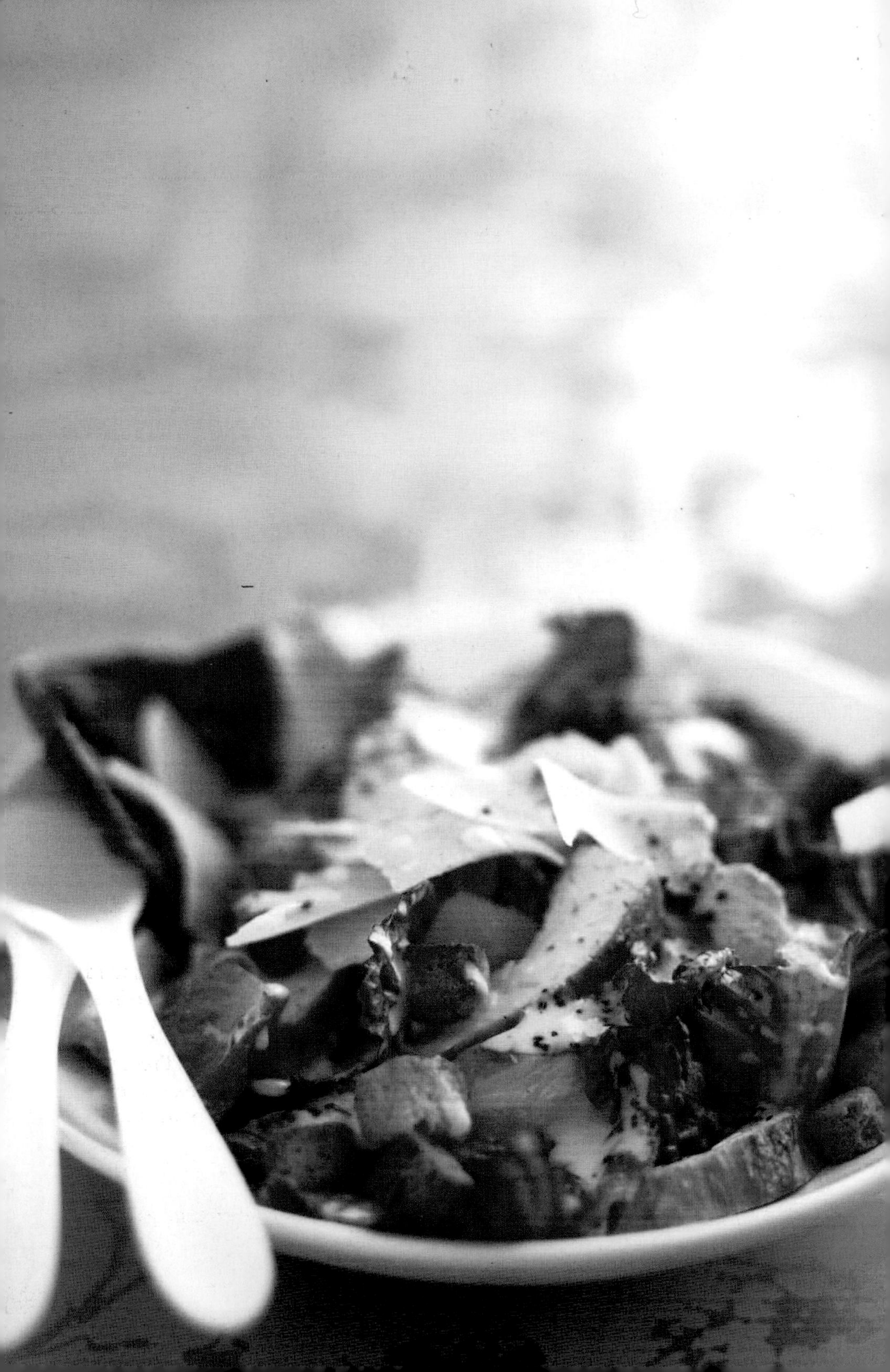

Chicken caesar salad

Serves 4
Ready in 25 minutes

3 skinless, boneless chicken breast fillets, about 450 g/1 lb in total

350 ml/12 fl oz/1⅓ cups chicken or vegetable stock

3 sprigs of fresh tarragon

3 black peppercorns

8 thin slices of French bread

20 ml/1½ tbsp olive oil

1 small garlic clove, crushed

5 ml/1 tsp Dijon mustard

10 ml/2 tsp sherry vinegar or white wine vinegar

60 ml/4 tbsp plain low-fat yoghurt

A pinch of caster (superfine) sugar

2.5 ml/½ tsp anchovy essence (extract) or Worcestershire sauce

1 Cos lettuce, torn into bite-sized pieces

15 g/½ oz Parmesan cheese shavings

1 Put the chicken breasts in a shallow pan in a single layer and pour the stock over. Lightly crush the tarragon to release the aromatic oils and add to the pan with the peppercorns. Slowly bring to the boil, then lower the heat, cover the pan with a lid and gently simmer for 15 minutes or until the chicken is cooked and tender.

2 Remove the chicken from the stock and cool slightly, then cut into bite-sized pieces.

3 Meanwhile, preheat the grill (broiler) to moderate. Very lightly brush the bread with half the oil, then cut the slices into 1 cm/½ in cubes. Place on the grill pan in a single layer and grill for 5–8 minutes, turning frequently, until the cubes are golden-brown all over. Set aside to cool.

4 To make the dressing, whisk together the remaining oil, the garlic, mustard, vinegar, yoghurt, sugar and anchovy essence or Worcestershire sauce in a bowl or shake them in a screw-topped jar.

5 Put the chicken and lettuce in a bowl and drizzle with half of the dressing. Gently mix together. Add the croutons and mix again. Drizzle the rest of the dressing over and scatter the Parmesan shavings on top. Serve at once.

Tip

★ Other ingredients such as sliced celery or chicory or cooked thin green beans can be added to the salad.

chicken
&
turkey

Lean, healthy and versatile, chicken and turkey have a lower saturated fat content than most red meats, but the amount of fat depends on which cut you choose and how you prepare and cook it. Chicken breast without skin, for example, contains 1.1 g fat per 100 g; the dark meat from a leg or thigh from the same bird, without skin, contains 2.5 g per 100 g, and chicken breast eaten with the skin a massive 13.8 g per 100 g.

To minimise the saturated fat content of poultry, roast or grill (broil) the meat with little or no added oil and remove the skin before serving or eating (the skin will keep the meat moist during cooking and adds very little to the total fat content of the meat).

Take care when buying commercial chicken and turkey products; coating in breadcrumbs or batter and deep-frying adds a huge amount of fat. Burgers and sausages made from poultry usually have added fat, so are unlikely to be any healthier than those made from red meat.

Included in this chapter are family favourites such as Griddled Turkey Goujons with Tarragon and Mustard Dip (see page 56) and more exotic dishes like Kashmiri Chicken (see page 43) and Caribbean Chicken with Sweet Potatoes (see page 47).

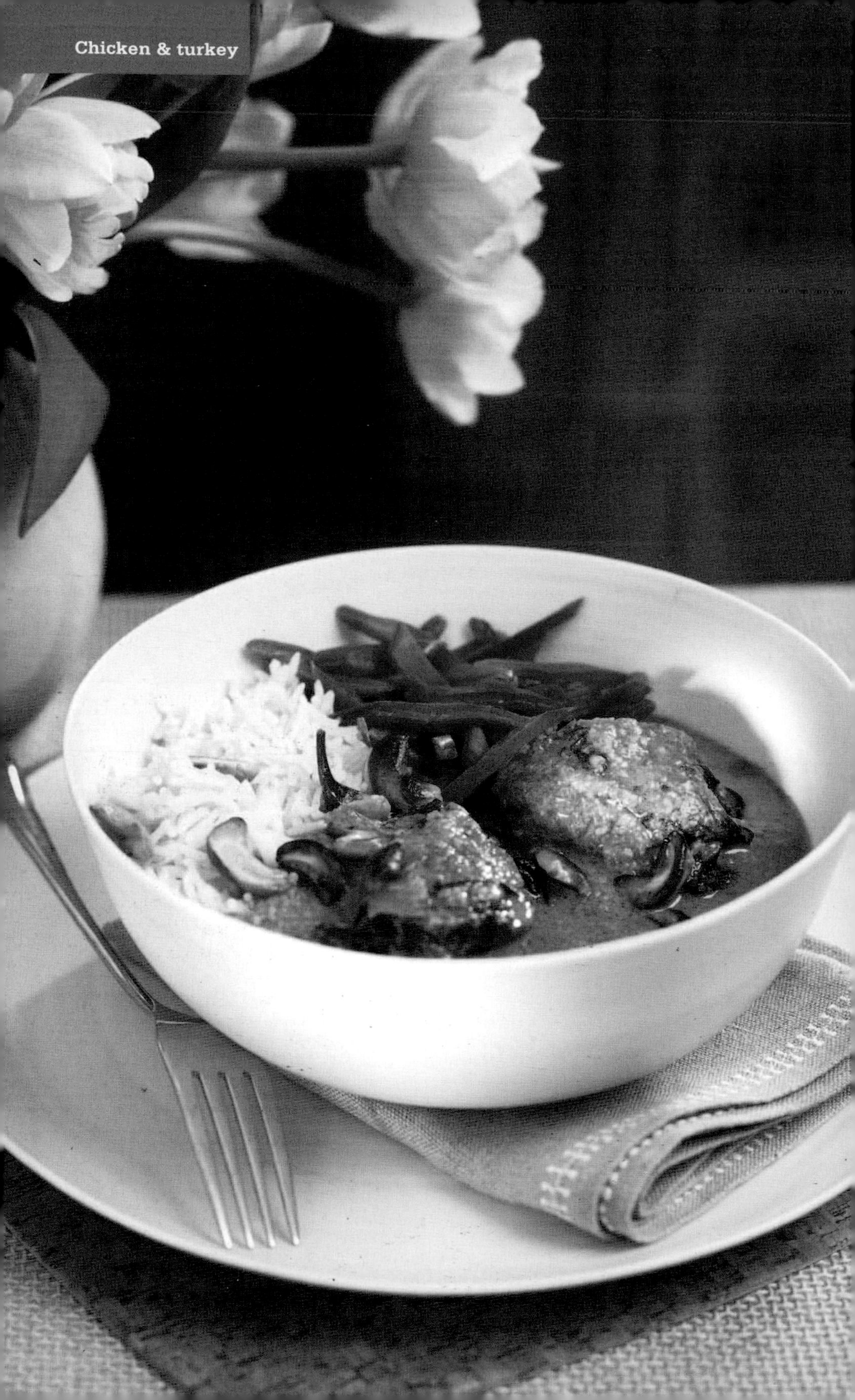

Kashmiri chicken

Serves 4
Ready in 30 minutes

50 g/2 oz/½ cup cashew nuts

1 onion, chopped

250 ml/8 fl oz/1 cup vegetable or chicken stock

2 garlic cloves, crushed

10 ml/2 tsp ground coriander

5 ml/1 tsp ground cumin

2.5 ml/½ tsp ground turmeric

2.5 ml/½ tsp ground ginger

4 skinless, boneless chicken breasts, cut into large cubes

10 ml/2 tsp cornflour (cornstarch)

300 ml/½ pint/1¼ cups thick plain yoghurt

150 ml/¼ pint/⅔ cup reduced-fat coconut milk

Salt and freshly ground black pepper

50 g/2 oz frozen leaf spinach, thawed

1 Dry-fry the nuts in a non-stick pan for 2–3 minutes, stirring frequently, until lightly browned. Tip the nuts on to a plate and set aside.

2 Place the onion in the pan with 100 ml/3½ fl oz/scant ½ cup of the stock. Cover and bring to the boil, then simmer for 2 minutes. Uncover and boil for about 5 minutes or until the stock has reduced entirely. Lower the heat and stir the onions until they are just beginning to colour. Stir in the garlic, coriander, cumin, turmeric, ginger and chicken and cook for 1 minute.

3 Blend the cornflour with the yoghurt, then add to the chicken mixture a tablespoonful at a time. Stir in the coconut milk and the remaining stock and season with salt and pepper. Half-cover with a lid and cook over a low heat for 12 minutes.

4 Stir in the spinach and cook for a further 3–4 minutes or until the chicken is cooked and tender. Spoon into warm bowls or deep plates and scatter with the toasted cashew nuts.

Serve with: Boiled or steamed basmati rice and green beans

Tip

★ Instead of the dry spices, you could use 1–2 tsp/5–10 ml of kashmiri or your favourite curry paste.

Chicken salad wraps

Serves 4
Ready in 20 minutes

3 skinless, boneless chicken breasts or a 400 g/14 oz pack of mini chicken fillets

15 ml/1 tbsp clear honey

10 ml/2 tsp fresh or bottled lemon juice

5 ml/1 tsp ground paprika

5 ml/1 tsp mustard seeds

10 ml/2 tsp sunflower oil

1 red (bell) pepper, halved, seeded and cut into strips

1 orange or yellow pepper, halved, seeded and cut into strips

Salt and freshly ground black pepper

4 soft flour tortilla wraps, each about 20 cm/8 in in diameter

30 ml/2 tbsp reduced-fat mayonnaise

150 g/5 oz bag of baby salad leaves

4 spring onions (scallions), trimmed and thinly sliced

Wedges of lemon to garnish (optional)

1 Trim the chicken breasts or fillets, if necessary, and cut into strips about 1 cm/½ in wide.

2 Mix together the honey, lemon juice, paprika and mustard seeds in a bowl. Add the strips of chicken and toss to coat. Leave to marinate for a few minutes or, if time allows, cover and chill in the fridge for 2 hours.

3 Heat the oil in a large non-stick frying pan. Add the marinated chicken and the pepper strips and fry over a high heat for 5–6 minutes, stirring frequently, until the chicken is lightly browned and cooked and the peppers are tender. Season to taste with salt and pepper and set aside.

4 Thinly spread each tortilla with 7.5 ml/1½ tsp of the mayonnaise. Scatter a handful of baby salad leaves and some spring onion slices down the centre of each, then top with the chicken and pepper mixture. Roll up, then cut each in half and serve with the rest of the salad leaves and a wedge of lemon to squeeze over the tortilla, if liked.

Tip

★ To make the tortillas easier to roll up, you can warm them, one at time for just a few seconds on each side, in a dry non-stick frying pan. Alternatively, pierce the packet and microwave them on High for 30 seconds.

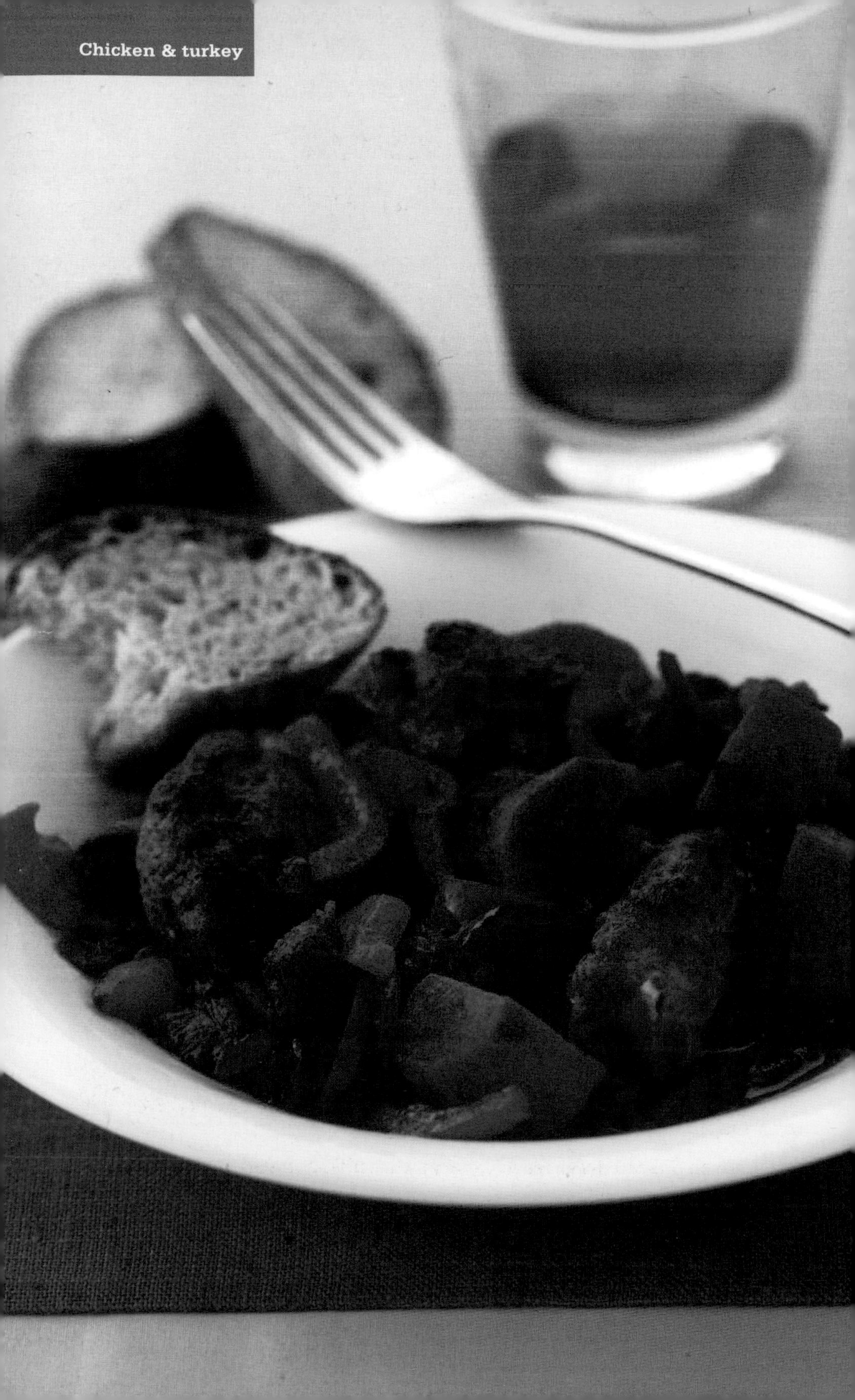

Caribbean chicken
with sweet potatoes

Serves 4
Ready in 30 minutes

8 chicken thighs

20 ml/1½ tbsp bought or home-made Caribbean seasoning (see below)

10 ml/2 tsp sunflower oil

200 g/7 oz frozen sliced mixed (bell) peppers

450 g/1 lb sweet potatoes, peeled and cut into 2 cm/¾ in chunks

400 g/14 oz/large can of chopped tomatoes

250 ml/8 fl oz/1 cup vegetable or chicken stock

Salt

1 Skin the chicken thighs, then cut each in half, removing and discarding the bone. Toss the meat in the seasoning.

2 Heat the oil in a large non-stick frying pan, add the chicken and cook over a moderate heat for 3–4 minutes, turning frequently, until lightly browned all over.

3 Add the mixed peppers and sweet potatoes and cook for 1 more minute, stirring, then add the tomatoes and stock.

4 Bring to the boil, then lower the heat. Cover the pan with a lid and simmer gently for 15–20 minutes or until the chicken and sweet potatoes are tender. Taste and add salt, if necessary.

Serve with: Crusty French bread

Tips

★ To make Caribbean seasoning for this dish, mix together 5 ml/1 tsp of ground coriander, 2.5 ml/½ tsp each of ground turmeric, ground ginger and ground cinnamon, and 1.5 ml/¼ tsp each of dry mustard powder, ground cumin, ground allspice and dried thyme.

★ If liked, use 2 fresh peppers instead of frozen ones. Halve and seed them, then cut into slices.

★ If you prefer a thicker sauce, simmer the chicken mixture uncovered for the last 10 minutes.

★ Sweet potatoes are very low in fat and provide vitamins C and E as well as potassium and fibre. Orange-fleshed varieties are a good source of beta-carotene.

Chicken skewers
with couscous

Serves 4
Ready in 25 minutes

10 ml/2 tsp olive oil

15 ml/1 tbsp lemon juice

5 ml/1 tsp clear honey

1 small garlic clove, crushed

2 large skinless, boneless chicken breasts, cut into 2 cm/¾ in cubes

A large sprig of fresh rosemary

1 courgette (zucchini), cut into 2 cm/¾ in slices

1 yellow (bell) pepper, halved, seeded and cut into 2 cm/¾ in pieces

1 green pepper, halved, seeded and cut into 2 cm/¾ in pieces

100 g/4 oz small plum tomatoes

Salt and freshly ground black pepper

For the couscous:

400 ml/14 fl oz/1¾ cups hot vegetable stock or water

2.5 ml/½ tsp dried Mediterranean herbs or thyme

250 g/9 oz/1½ cups couscous

1 Whisk together the oil, lemon juice, honey and garlic in a bowl, add the chicken and mix together. Bruise the rosemary sprig with a rolling pin and tuck under the chicken. Marinate at room temperature for at least 10 minutes, or cover and marinate in the fridge for an hour or two.

2 When ready to cook, add the vegetables and tomatoes to the chicken, season lightly and mix together to coat everything in the marinade.

3 Preheat the grill (broiler) to moderately hot and line the grill pan with foil. Thread the chicken and vegetables on to eight metal or soaked wooden skewers and grill for 10–15 minutes, turning from time to time.

4 Meanwhile, pour the stock or water into a saucepan (add a pinch of salt if using water). Add the dried herbs and bring to the boil. Pour in the couscous in a steady stream and stir well. Turn off the heat, cover and leave to stand for 5 minutes. When ready to serve, heat gently for 1 minute, stirring with a fork to separate the grains. Serve with the kebabs.

Tip

★ Try adding some thawed frozen peas to the boiling stock when stirring in the couscous.

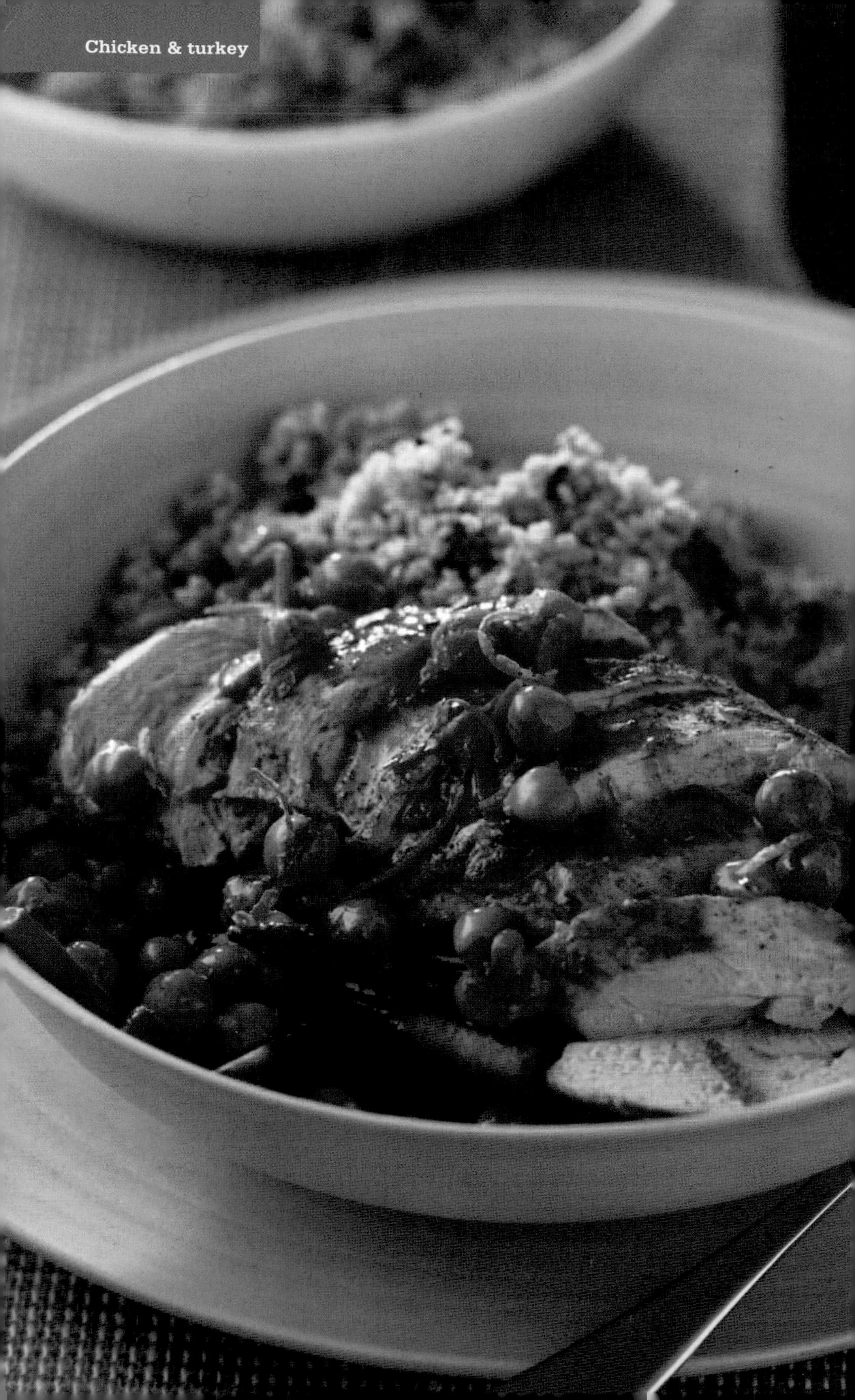

Moroccan chicken

Serves 4
Ready in 40 minutes

For the chicken:
10 ml/2 tsp olive oil
4 skinless, boneless chicken breasts, about 175 g/6 oz each, trimmed
1 shallot, very finely chopped
150 ml/¼ pint/⅔ cup hot chicken or vegetable stock
45 ml/3 tbsp dry white wine, or extra stock
10 ml/2 tsp fresh or bottled grated root ginger
2.5 ml/½ tsp each ground coriander, ground cumin and ground cinnamon
1 lemon
400 g/14 oz/large can of chick peas (garbanzos), drained and rinsed
Salt and freshly ground black pepper
For the couscous:
400 ml/14 fl oz/1¾ cups hot vegetable stock or water with a pinch of salt
A pinch of dried chilli flakes
250 g/9 oz/1½ cups couscous
30 ml/2 tbsp chopped fresh coriander (cilantro), optional

1 Heat the oil in a non-stick frying pan and fry the chicken for 3–4 minutes, turning once, until golden. Remove from the pan, leaving any juices.

2 Add the shallot with 45 ml/3 tbsp of the stock. Cover and cook for 3–4 minutes, then uncover, add the wine or extra stock and cook until most of the liquid has evaporated. Stir in the ginger and spices and cook for 1 minute.

3 Remove and reserve a few fine strips of zest from the lemon. Finely grate the remainder and squeeze the juice. Add all but 15 ml/1 tbsp of the juice to the pan with the grated zest. Add the chicken breasts, chick peas and remaining stock. Season with salt and pepper.

4 Bring to the boil, then cover tightly, reduce the heat and simmer gently for 12–15 minutes or until the chicken is cooked and tender.

5 Meanwhile, to cook the couscous pour the stock or salted water into a saucepan. Add the chilli flakes and bring to the boil. Pour in the couscous and stir well. Turn off the heat, cover and leave to stand for 5 minutes.

6 Stir the coriander into the couscous, if using, then heat gently for 1 minute, stirring and separating the grains. Slice the chicken and arrange on a bed of couscous. Spoon the sauce over and scatter with the reserved lemon zest.

Serve with: Steamed green beans

Warm chicken salad

Serves 4
Ready in 20 minutes

1 garlic clove, crushed

5 ml/1 tsp fresh or bottled grated root ginger

15 ml/1 tbsp light soy sauce

10 ml/2 tsp sunflower oil

3 skinless, boneless chicken breasts, about 175 g/6 oz each, cut into cubes

30 ml/2 tbsp pumpkin seeds

100 g/4 oz cherry or baby plum tomatoes, halved

4 spring onions (scallions), trimmed and diagonally sliced

2.5 ml/½ tsp finely grated orange zest

30 ml/2 tbsp orange juice

2.5 ml/½ tsp Dijon mustard

Salt and freshly ground black pepper

100 g/4 oz bag of herb salad or baby salad leaves

1 Whisk together the garlic, ginger, soy sauce and oil in a bowl. Add the chicken and turn to coat on all sides.

2 Dry-fry the pumpkin seeds in a non-stick frying pan for 2–3 minutes, then remove and set aside.

3 Add the chicken to the pan and stir fry for 3–4 minutes. Stir in the tomatoes, spring onions and any remaining marinade, then cook for 2–3 minutes or until the chicken pieces are cooked and the spring onions just tender.

4 Blend together the orange zest, juice and mustard. Add to the pan and stir until everything is coated. Season to taste, then turn off the heat.

5 Put the salad leaves in a serving bowl, then spoon the chicken mixture over with any pan juices. Scatter with the toasted pumpkin seeds and serve straight away.

Tips

★ A lime dressing also works well for this salad. Instead of orange zest and juice, use lime zest and juice mixed with 5 ml/1 tsp of clear honey.

★ Although all seeds and nuts are fairly high in fat, they are nutritional powerhouses and should be included in the diet in moderation. Pumpkin seeds contain beneficial oils and are richer in iron than any other seed; they are also an excellent source of zinc, contain a good amount of beta-carotene and several other antioxidants.

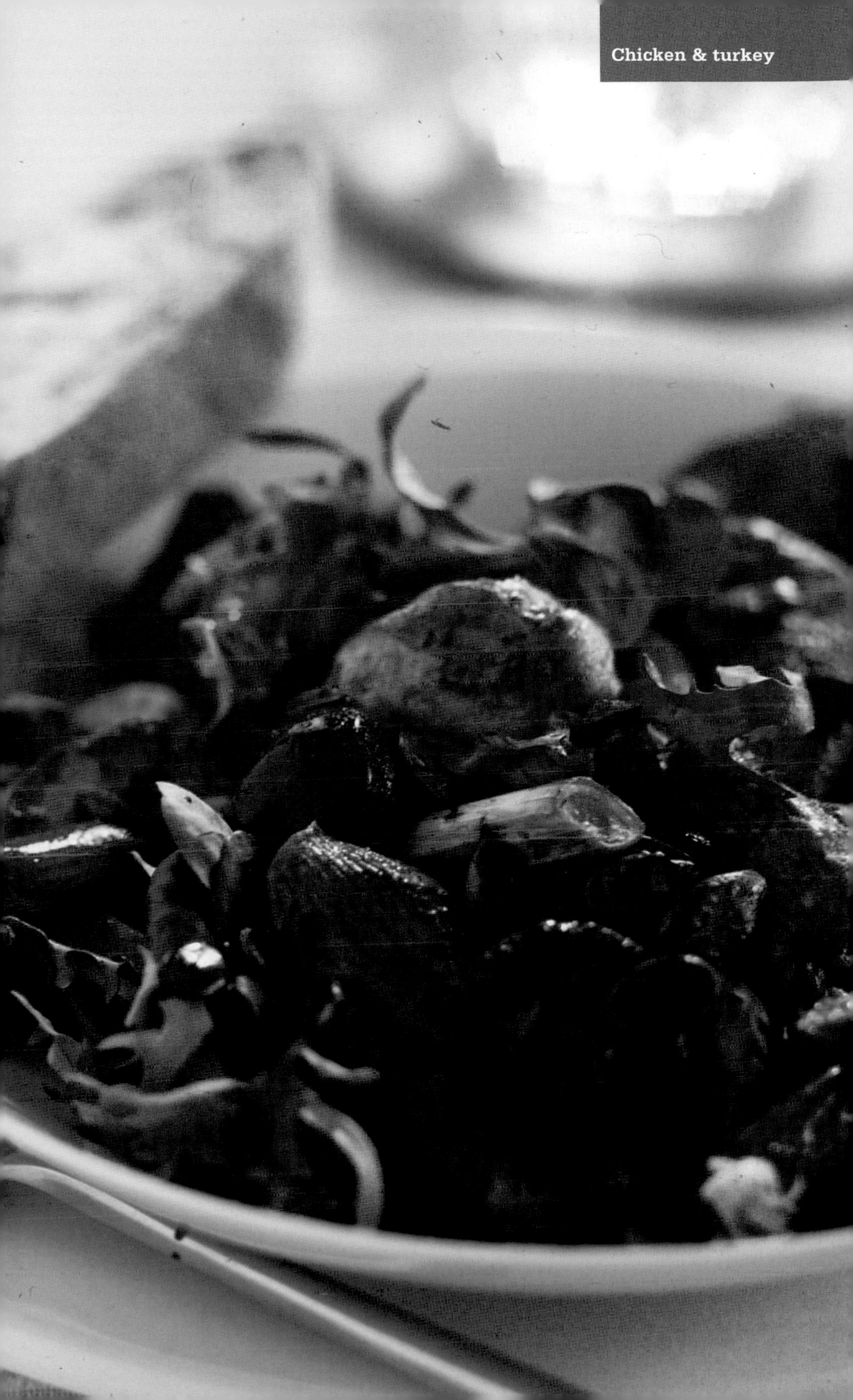

Chilli and lime
spatchcocked poussins

Serves 4
Ready in 40 minutes

45 ml/3 tbsp clear honey

30 ml/2 tbsp dark soy sauce

30 ml/2 tbsp sweet chilli sauce

5 ml/1 tsp Dijon mustard

Finely grated zest and juice of 1 lime

2 spatchcocked poussins (Cornish hens), each about 750 g/1¾ lb

1 red chilli, halved, seeded and finely chopped

30 ml/2 tbsp chopped fresh coriander (cilantro)

Salt and freshly ground black pepper

1 Preheat the grill (broiler) to medium and line the grill pan with foil. Mix together the honey, soy sauce, chilli sauce, mustard, lime zest and juice in a small bowl. Reserve 30 ml/2 tbsp of the glaze, then brush the poussins with some of the remaining glaze.

2 Place the poussins, skin-sides down, on the grill rack and grill (broil) for 15 minutes. Turn the poussins, brush with more glaze and grill for a further 12 minutes.

3 Stir the chilli and coriander into the reserved glaze and season with a little salt and pepper. Brush over the poussins and grill for 3–4 more minutes or until the poussins are cooked through and the juices from the thigh run clear when pierced with a skewer or thin knife.

4 Transfer the poussins to a board and cover with foil. Leave to rest for 5 minutes, then remove any skewers and cut each one in two along the length of the breastbone.

Serve with: A green salad and slices of lime to squeeze over the poussin

Tips

★ Spatchcooked poussins are split, flattened and held in position with skewers to allow them to be grilled evenly. If the poussins start to brown too quickly during cooking, lower the position of the grill pan.

★ Most of the fat in poultry is in the skin, so this should be removed before eating.

Griddled turkey gougons
with tarragon and mustard dip

 Serves 4
Ready in 20 minutes

450 g/1 lb turkey escalopes
5 ml/1 tsp olive oil
Finely grated zest and juice of 1 lime
10 ml/2 tsp Cajun spice mix
Salt and freshly ground black pepper
200 g/7 oz bag of mixed salad leaves
For the dip:
150 ml/¼ pint/⅔ cup low-fat yoghurt
60 ml/4 tbsp chopped fresh tarragon
15 ml/1 tbsp Dijon mustard

1 Trim the turkey escalopes if necessary, then cut into thick strips.

2 Mix together the oil, lime zest and juice, spice mix and salt and pepper in a bowl. Add the turkey strips and leave to marinate for about 10 minutes.

3 Meanwhile, to make the dip, mix together all the ingredients and season to taste with a little salt and pepper. Set aside.

4 Heat a ridged cast-iron grill (broiler) pan or non-stick frying pan. Add the turkey strips and cook over a moderately high heat for 3–4 minutes on all sides or until thoroughly cooked; take care not to overcook, though, or the turkey will loose its succulence.

5 Arrange the salad leaves on four plates and divide the griddled turkey strips between them. Serve while still hot, accompanied by the tarragon and mustard dip.

Serve with: Crusty French bread, sliced ciabatta or wholemeal rolls

Tips

★ Spice and seasoning mixes add lots of flavour to dishes with virtually no fat. Cajun spice mix includes chillies, garlic, ground ginger, allspice, coriander seed, ground cumin, fennel, cardamom, mustard, thyme, sage and oregano.

★ Fresh tuna steaks are delicious prepared in the same way, slicing into strips once grilled.

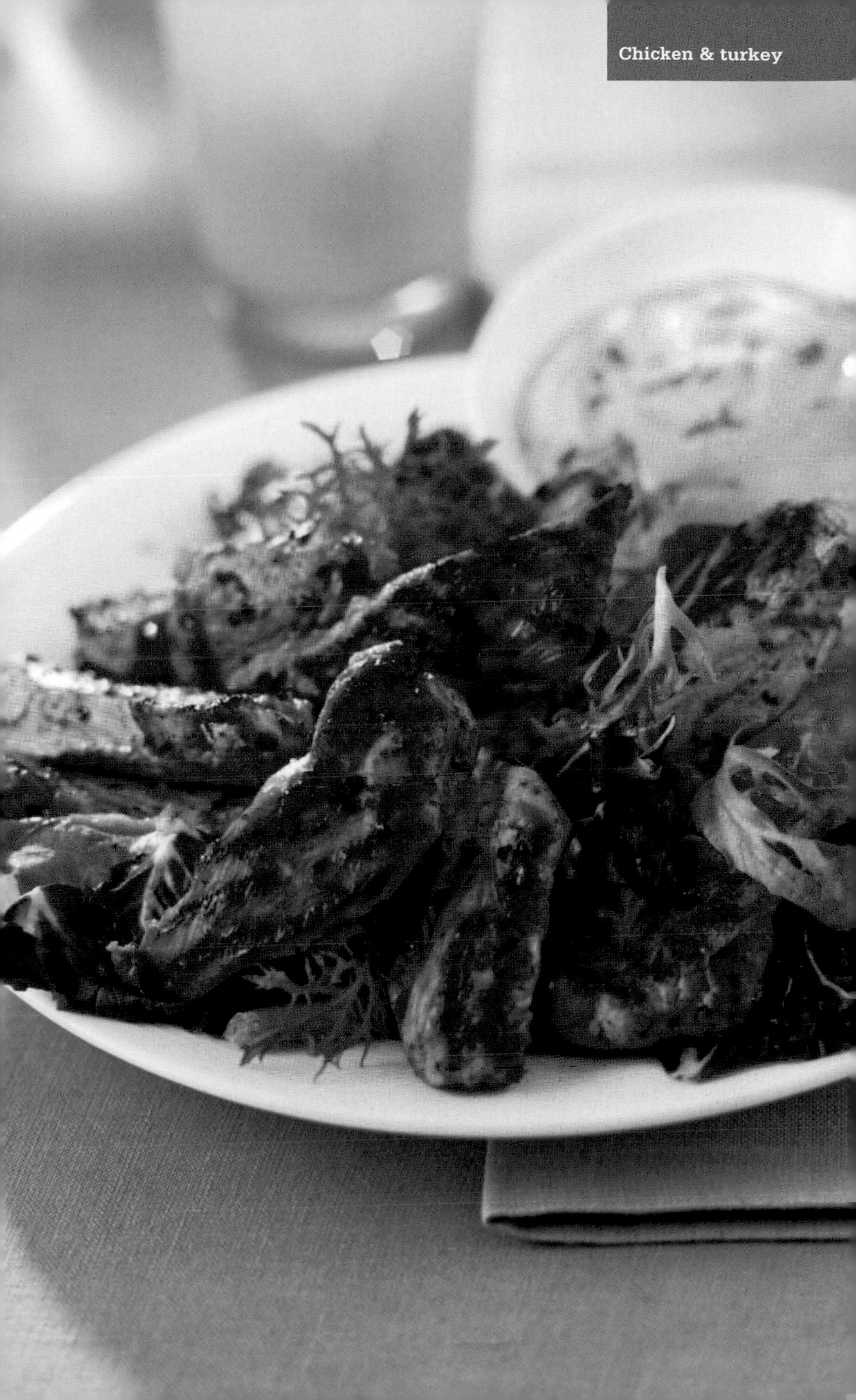

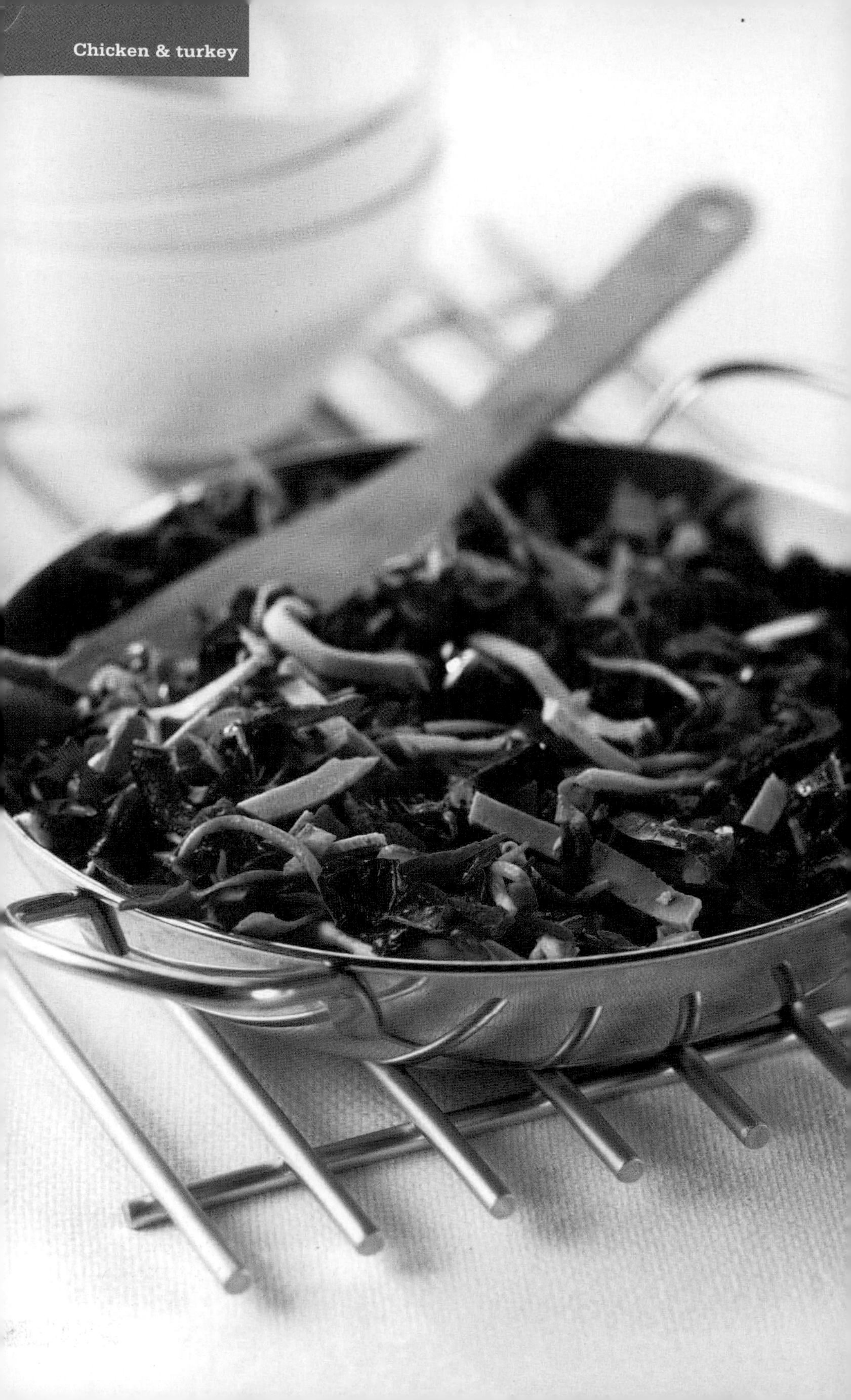

Turkey and tagliatelle
sauté

Serves 4
Ready in 25 minutes

175 g/6 oz tagliatelle or pappardelle, broken into short strips

10 ml/2 tsp toasted sesame oil

350 g/12 oz turkey escalopes, cut into thin slices

1 red (bell) pepper, halved, seeded and sliced

60 ml/4 tbsp chicken or vegetable stock

2 large carrots, peeled and coarsely grated

100 g/4 oz small ripe tomatoes, quartered

50 g/2 oz fresh baby spinach leaves

Salt and freshly ground black pepper

1 Bring a pan of lightly salted water to the boil and add the pasta. Bring back to the boil, half-cover the pan with a lid and cook for 8–10 minutes or according to packet instructions until just tender. Drain in a colander.

2 Meanwhile, heat the oil in a wok or non-stick frying pan, add the turkey and stir-fry over a medium-high heat for 3–4 minutes until golden-brown. Lift out of the pan with a slotted spoon, leaving any juices behind, and set aside on a plate.

3 Add the pepper slices and half the stock to the pan and cook for 2 minutes. Add the carrots and tomatoes and cook for a further minute, then stir in the spinach leaves.

4 Return the turkey to the pan with the remaining stock and season with salt and pepper. Cook, stirring, for 1 minute or until the spinach wilts and the vegetables are tender.

5 Add the pasta to the pan and cook, stirring gently occasionally, for a few seconds or until warmed through. Spoon on to warm plates and serve straight away.

Tips

★ Prepare all the ingredients before you start to cook; once stir-frying starts, there's no time for chopping and slicing.

★ Stir-frying is one of the healthiest methods of cooking as you need only a little oil. Toasted sesame seed oil adds a delicious distinctive nutty flavour to this dish, but you can substitute sunflower oil if you prefer.

beef,
pork
&
lamb

Beef, pork, lamb and venison are wonderfully flavourful and can be cooked in a huge number of delicious ways to suit every taste and occasion from family meals to elegant suppers when entertaining. Meat is an excellent concentrated source of protein and contains many essential nutrients. It is often considered to be high in saturated fat, but modern breeding techniques have improved this and now only about half the fat in meat is saturated; the rest is mainly monounsaturated.

You can further reduce the fat in meat-based dishes by choosing well-trimmed lean joints and cuts, by trimming off visible fat from chops and steaks and by using a minimal amount of added fat when cooking.

Some recipes such as Spicy Beef and Broccoli (see page 64) and Chinese-style Pork (see page 72) are incredibly quick to prepare; others, such as Mustard Roast Beef (see page 67) and Greek Lamb Casserole (see page 83) take longer to cook but need little preparation – they are simply popped in the oven and left to cook to perfection.

Quick chilli beef

Serves 4
Ready in 30 minutes

350 g/12 oz lean minced (ground) beef

1 onion, chopped

1 garlic clove, crushed

5 ml/1 tsp ground cumin

5 ml/1 tsp mild chilli powder

400 g/14 oz/large can of chopped tomatoes

15 ml/1 tbsp sun-dried tomato purée (paste)

5 ml/1 tsp dried mixed herbs

225 g/8 oz button mushrooms, quartered

400 g/14 oz/large can of red kidney beans, drained and rinsed

200 g/7 oz/small can of sweetcorn, drained

250 ml/8 fl oz/1 cup beef stock

Salt and freshly ground black pepper

30 ml/2 tbsp chopped fresh coriander (cilantro) or parsley (optional)

1 Put the beef and onion in a non-stick pan and cook for 3–4 minutes over a moderately high heat, stirring to break up the beef, until well-browned.

2 Add the garlic, cumin and chilli powder and cook for a further minute, then stir in the tomatoes, tomato purée, herbs, mushrooms, beans, sweetcorn and stock. Season with salt and pepper and bring to the boil.

3 Turn down the heat, half-cover the pan and simmer for 25 minutes, stirring occasionally, until the beef and vegetables are tender. Spoon into warm bowls and garnish with chopped coriander or parsley, if liked.

Serve with: Steamed or boiled rice and reduced-fat guacamole

Tips

★ Instead of rice, serve with a crisp breadcrumb topping. Simmer for just 15 minutes, then transfer to a flameproof casserole dish (Dutch oven) or ovenproof baking dish. Sprinkle with 100 g/4 oz/2 cups of coarse fresh breadcrumbs and bake in a preheated oven at 200°C/400°F/gas 6/fan oven 180°C for 15 minutes or until the topping is golden.

★ Kidney beans are low in fat and rich in carbohydrate. They provide vitamin B and a useful amount of iron. They are also a good source of soluble fibre, which fills you up and may help to reduce high cholesterol levels.

Spicy beef and broccoli

Serves 4
Ready in 25 minutes

350 g/12 oz rump steak, trimmed

30 ml/2 tbsp cornflour (cornstarch)

7.5 ml/1½ tsp Chinese five-spice powder

Salt and freshly ground black pepper

10 ml/2 tsp sunflower oil

120 ml/4 fl oz/½ cup beef or vegetable stock

1 red onion, very thinly sliced

2 large carrots, peeled and cut into matchsticks

175 g/6 oz broccoli, divided into small florets

2 x 150 g/5 oz packets of straight-to-wok medium or thick noodles

15 ml/1 tbsp dark soy sauce

2.5 ml/½ tsp dried chilli flakes

1 Slice the beef across the grain, then cut the slices into long, fine strips. Mix together the cornflour, five-spice powder and a little salt and pepper in a bowl, add the beef strips and stir to coat lightly.

2 Heat the oil in a wok or large non-stick frying pan, add the beef and cook for 1–2 minutes over a high heat until lightly browned. Remove with a slotted spoon and set aside.

3 Pour the stock into the wok or frying pan and heat until bubbling. Add the onion, cover the pan with a lid and simmer for 3 minutes, then remove the lid and cook for a further minute. Stir in the carrots and broccoli and continue to cook uncovered for 3–4 minutes or until the stock has reduced by about half and the vegetables are nearly tender.

4 Mix in the noodles and soy sauce and heat through for 2 minutes, then divide between four warm plates.

5 Return the beef to the pan and add the chilli flakes. Turn up the heat a little and cook for about 45 seconds until hot. Spoon the beef on top of the noodles and serve.

Tip

★ Instead of straight-to-wok noodles, you could use 200 g/7 oz of thick egg noodles. Cook in boiling stock or water for 3–4 minutes, then drain well before adding to the pan.

★ Instead of rump steak, try 'stir-fry' beef strips or 'minute' steak, pork fillet or chicken breast.

Mustard roast beef

Serves 4
Ready in 1½–2¾ hours

1 topside of beef joint, about 1 kg/2¼ lb

30 ml/2 tbsp Dijon mustard

25 ml/1½ tbsp olive oil

Salt and freshly ground black pepper

500 g/18 oz potatoes, peeled and cut into bite-size chunks

2 courgettes (zucchini), cut into large chunks

1 onion, thickly sliced

2 red onions, thickly sliced

1 Take the beef joint out of the fridge about half an hour before you are ready to cook to allow it to come up to room temperature. Preheat the oven to 180°C/350°F/gas 4/fan oven 160°C.

2 Mix the mustard with 10 ml/½ tbsp of the oil, then brush evenly all over the beef. Season with salt and pepper and place in a non-stick roasting tin. Roast the beef for 35 minutes if you prefer it medium-rare, 50 minutes if you like it medium and 1 hour if you prefer a well-done joint.

3 Turn up the oven temperature to 200°C/400°F/gas 6/fan oven 180°C. Toss the vegetables in the remaining oil until lightly coated and season with a little salt and pepper. Arrange around the joint of beef in the tin and roast for a further 35 minutes, turning the vegetables and basting the meat at least twice during cooking.

4 Remove the meat from the oven (leave the vegetables to roast for a further 10 minutes until well-browned and tender), place on a board and cover with foil. Leave for 10 minutes before carving to allow the temperature to even out and the meat to rest, making it easier to carve.

5 Remove the string and carve the beef into thin slices. Serve with the roasted vegetables and some gravy, if liked.

Tip

★ Also known as top rump, topside is usually sold boned and rolled ready for roasting (ask the butcher to do this for you if necessary). It is a very lean joint, so make sure you baste it frequently with the meat juices during cooking to keep it moist.

Seared beef with herb and horseradish mash

Serves 4
Ready in 30 minutes

750 g/1¾ lb thin sirloin or rump steak

30 ml/2 tbsp dark soy sauce

30 ml/2 tbsp dry sherry

15 ml/1 tbsp clear honey

1 garlic clove, crushed

750 g/1¾ lb potatoes, peeled and cut into large chunks

1 red (bell) pepper, halved, seeded and cut into thick strips

1 yellow (bell) pepper, halved, seeded and cut into thick strips

75 ml/5 tbsp reduced-fat crème fraîche

15 ml/1 tbsp creamed horseradish

45 ml/3 tbsp chopped fresh parsley

30 ml/2 tbsp snipped fresh chives

Salt and freshly ground black pepper

Snipped and whole fresh chives to garnish (optional)

1 Trim any fat off the steak and cut the meat across the grain into thick strips. Mix together the soy sauce, sherry, honey and garlic in a bowl and add the beef. Stir to coat the strips and set aside for a few minutes.

2 Cook the potatoes in lightly salted boiling water for about 15 minutes or until tender.

3 Meanwhile, preheat the grill (broiler) to moderately hot and line the grill pan with foil. Divide the meat and pepper strips into four portions and thread each set on to two metal or soaked wooden skewers. Place under the grill and cook for 4–5 minutes on each side or until the meat is well-browned but still moist and the peppers are lightly charred and tender.

4 Drain the potatoes thoroughly, then return to the pan and mash with 60 ml/4 tbsp of the crème fraîche until smooth. Add the remaining crème fraîche, the horseradish, parsley, chives and some salt and beat with a wooden spoon until light and fluffy. Cover the pan with the lid to keep warm.

5 Spoon the mash on to four warm serving plates and serve with the beef and pepper skewers. Garnish with fresh chives, if liked, and grind some black pepper over before serving.

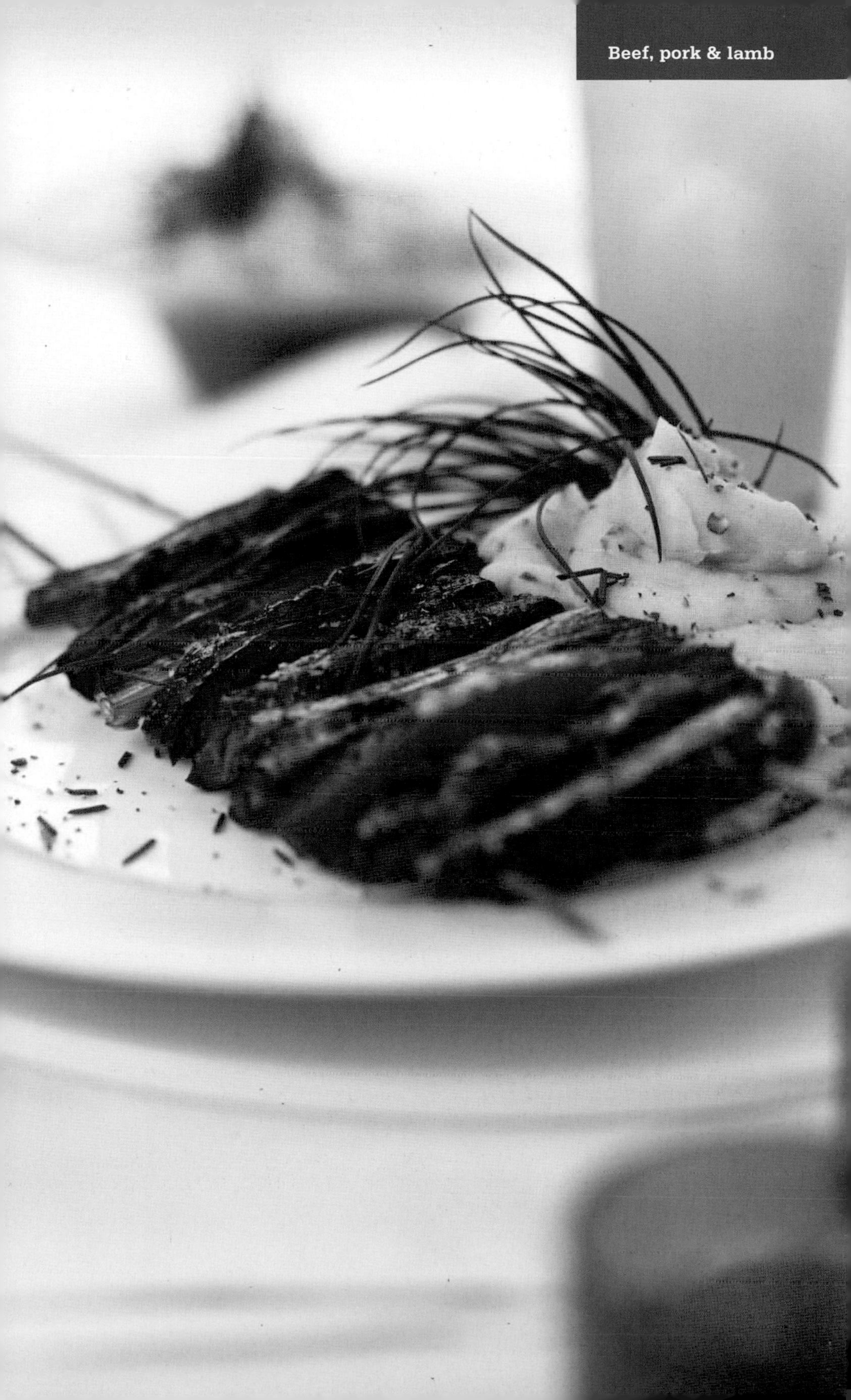

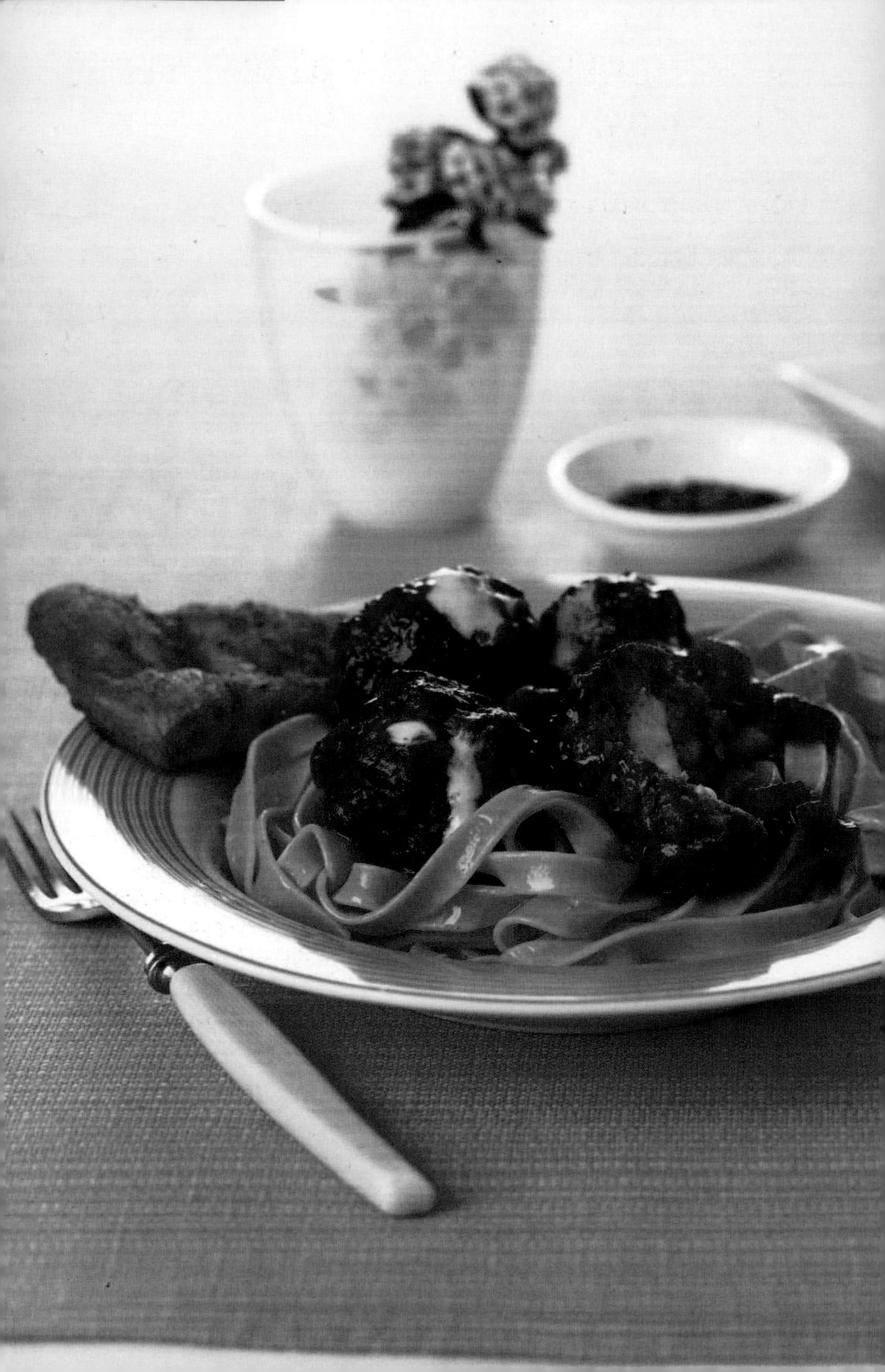

Mozzarella meatballs
in rich tomato sauce

Serves 4
Ready in 30 minutes

50 g/2 oz/1 cup fresh breadcrumbs

30 ml/2 tbsp chopped fresh parsley or 2.5 ml/½ tsp dried mixed herbs

15 ml/1 tbsp skimmed milk

175 g/6 oz lean minced (ground) beef

175 g/6 oz lean minced pork

1 small onion, very finely chopped

Salt and freshly ground black pepper

75 g/3 oz reduced-fat Mozzarella cheese, cut into 16 cubes

75 ml/5 tbsp dry white wine or vegetable stock

1 carrot, finely diced

1 celery stick, finely diced

1 garlic clove, crushed

400 g/14 oz/large can of chopped tomatoes

15 ml/1 tbsp sun-dried tomato purée (paste)

400 g/14 oz dried tagliatelle

1 Put the breadcrumbs and parsley or dried herbs in a bowl and sprinkle with the milk. Stir briefly with a fork. Add the minced meats, half of the chopped onion and some salt and pepper. Shape into 16 balls with damp hands. Push a Mozzarella cube into the centre of each meatball, enclosing the cheese completely with the meat. Chill in the fridge.

2 Put the remaining chopped onion in a pan with the wine or vegetable stock. Bring to the boil, cover and simmer for 5 minutes. Add the carrot, celery, garlic, tomatoes, tomato purée and some salt and pepper. Bring to a gentle simmer, half-cover the pan and cook for 15 minutes or until the vegetables are very tender and the sauce is thick.

3 Meanwhile, cook the tagliatelle in a large pan of lightly salted boiling water for 10–12 minutes or according to the packet instructions until *al dente* (tender but still firm to the bite).

4 While the sauce and tagliatelle are cooking, fry the meatballs in a large non-stick frying pan with no added fat for 10–12 minutes. Remove and drain on kitchen paper (paper towels). Drain the tagliatelle and serve topped with 4 meatballs and the tomato sauce.

Serve with: Herb-flavoured foccacia or ciabatta

Chinese-style pork

Serves 4
Ready in 25 minutes

400 g/14 oz lean minced (ground) pork
2 garlic cloves, crushed
2.5 cm/1 in piece of fresh root ginger, peeled and grated
1 large carrot, peeled and coarsely grated
1 red (bell) pepper, halved, seeded and diced
1 bunch of spring onions (scallions), sliced
5 ml/1 tsp cornflour (cornstarch)
30 ml/2 tbsp dark soy sauce
5 ml/1 tsp light brown sugar
120 ml/4 fl oz/½ cup vegetable stock
Freshly ground black pepper
200 g/7 oz/3½ cups beansprouts, rinsed
Whole Iceberg or other lettuce leaves

1 Heat a large non-stick frying pan or wok until hot. Add the pork and cook over a fairly high heat for 4–5 minutes until browned, stirring frequently to break up the meat.

2 Stir in the garlic, ginger, carrot, diced pepper and spring onions and cook for 2 more minutes.

3 Blend the cornflour with the soy sauce and sugar, then stir in the stock. Add to the pan and bring to the boil, stirring all the time. Season with pepper, then cover the pan with a lid and simmer for 2 minutes.

4 Add the beansprouts, then re-cover the pan and simmer for 3 more minutes or until the meat and vegetables are tender. Spoon the mixture into lettuce leaves and serve hot.

Serve with: Sweet chilli sauce and boiled rice

Tips

★ Always buy good-quality 'extra-lean' minced pork. If a lot of fat comes out of the meat during cooking, drain the meat after browning it in a sieve (strainer) over the sink, then return it to the pan. You could also ask your butcher to mince a lean piece of pork for this recipe.

★ Due to modern breeding techniques, pork is much leaner than it used to be and, providing you trim off any visible fat, is a really healthy choice. It's also an excellent source of the B vitamins and zinc.

Hot and spicy pork

Serves 4
Ready in 25 minutes

350 g/12 oz lean minced (ground) pork
150 g/5 oz button mushrooms, halved
1 red chilli, halved, seeded and finely chopped
A pinch of Chinese five-spice powder or ground allspice
100 ml/3½ fl oz/scant ½ cup vegetable stock
30 ml/2 tbsp sweet chilli or plum sauce
Salt and freshly ground black pepper
250 g/9 oz packet of rice noodles
2 spring onions (scallions), diagonally sliced

1 Heat a large non-stick frying pan or wok until hot. Add the pork and cook over a fairly high heat for 4–5 minutes or until well-browned, stirring frequently to break up the meat.

2 Add the mushrooms, chilli and five-spice powder or allspice to the pan. Cook for 1 more minute, stirring all the time.

3 Pour in the stock and add the chilli or plum sauce. Season the mixture with a little salt and pepper and bring to the boil. Turn down the heat and simmer for 15 minutes or until the meat and mushrooms are tender.

4 Meanwhile, cook the rice noodles in lightly salted boiling water for 3–4 minutes or according to the packet instructions until cooked. Drain and divide between four warm serving plates.

5 Spoon the pork mixture on top of the noodles and serve straight away, scattered with the spring onions.

Tip

★ Rice noodles are also known as cellophane noodles as they have a transparent appearance. Some only require soaking in boiling water to cook them, so check the packet instructions carefully. Instead of rice noodles, you could use a 250 g/9 oz packet of thick egg noodles.

Venison sausages
with red wine gravy

Serves 4
Ready in 30 minutes

10 ml/2 tsp olive oil

8 venison sausages

150 ml/¼ pint/⅔ cup hot beef or vegetable stock

2 shallots, finely chopped

1 garlic clove, finely chopped

150 ml/¼ pint/⅔ cup red wine

30 ml/2 tbsp redcurrant jelly

15 ml/1 tbsp chopped fresh thyme

Salt and freshly ground black pepper

1 Heat half the oil in a non-stick frying pan. Add the sausages and cook gently for 15 minutes, turning frequently, until browned all over. Transfer to kitchen paper (paper towels) to blot up excess fat. Wipe the pan clean.

2 Add the remaining oil and 45 ml/3 tbsp of the stock to the pan. Add the shallots and garlic and cook for 3–4 minutes or until all the stock has evaporated, then cook for a further minute until the shallots are beginning to brown.

3 Add the rest of the stock, the wine and the redcurrant jelly to the pan. Bring to the boil, stirring, until the jelly has melted. Simmer the mixture over a gentle heat for 5 minutes.

4 Return the sausages to the pan and add the thyme. Simmer for 2–3 minutes or until heated through. Taste the gravy and season to taste with salt and pepper.

Serve with: Mashed potatoes or polenta (see below) and a green vegetable such as beans

Tip

★ Polenta can be a delicious low-fat accompaniment for dishes with sauces and gravy. To serve 4, bring 900 ml/1½ pints/3¾ cups of vegetable stock to the boil. Pour in 175 g/6 oz/1½ cups of polenta in a steady stream, whisking well to prevent lumps forming. Cook over a gentle heat for 4–5 minutes, stirring with a wooden spoon, until soft and smooth. Taste and season with salt and pepper and stir in a little grated lemon zest, ground paprika or chopped fresh parsley, if liked.

Lamb kebabs with
cucumber and tomato salsa

Serves 4
Ready in 25 minutes

For the kebabs:
700 g/1½ lb lean lamb
Juice of ½ lime
15 ml/1 tbsp olive oil
A large pinch of dried oregano
1 garlic clove, crushed
A pinch of ground paprika, plus extra for sprinkling
8 oval wholemeal or white pitta breads
150 ml/¼ pint/⅔ cup plain yoghurt
For the salsa:
Finely grated zest of 1 lime
Juice of ½ lime
5 ml/1 tsp clear honey
Salt and freshly ground black pepper
½ cucumber, diced
225 g/8 oz plum tomatoes, seeded and diced

1 To make the kebabs, trim any fat off the lamb and cut the meat into bite-sized pieces.

2 Whisk together the lime juice, oil, oregano, garlic and paprika. Add the lamb, cover and marinate for 10 minutes at room temperature or, if time allows, for 2–3 hours in the fridge.

3 Meanwhile, to make the salsa, whisk together the lime zest, juice and honey in a bowl and season with salt and pepper. Add the cucumber and tomatoes and stir to coat. Set aside until ready to serve.

4 Preheat the grill (broiler) to medium-high and line the grill pan with foil. Thread the lamb on to eight metal or soaked wooden skewers and grill for 4–5 minutes on each side or until cooked to your liking.

5 Meanwhile, toast the pitta breads in a hot ridged cast-iron pan or in the toaster. Serve 2 pittas each with 2 kebabs, some cucumber and tomato salsa and a few spoonfuls of yoghurt.

Simple lamb hotpot

Serves 4
Ready in 2 hours

4 boneless lean lamb leg steaks, about 500 g/18 oz in total
10 ml/2 tsp sunflower oil
2 large onions, peeled and very thinly sliced
600 ml/1 pint/2½ cups lamb or vegetable stock
5 ml/1 tsp fresh thyme leaves or 2.5 ml/½ tsp dried
4 large baking potatoes, peeled and thinly sliced
4 carrots, peeled and sliced
Salt and freshly ground black pepper

1 Preheat the oven to 180°C/350°F/gas 4/fan oven 160°C. Trim any fat from the lamb and cut the meat into 2 cm/¾ in cubes.

2 Heat the oil in a non-stick frying pan, add the lamb and fry over a high heat for 2–3 minutes, turning frequently, until well-browned all over. Remove from the pan and set aside.

3 Add the onions to the pan with 45 ml/3 tbsp of the stock. Cook over a high heat for 2–3 minutes, stirring frequently, until all the stock has evaporated. Turn off the heat and stir in the thyme.

4 Place half the onions, half the potatoes and half the carrots in a deep casserole dish (Dutch oven), seasoning with salt and pepper. Place the lamb on top of the vegetables, then top with the remaining vegetables, seasoning as you go and finishing with a layer of potatoes.

5 Pour almost all the remaining stock over and cover with a tight-fitting lid or a piece of foil. Cook for 1 hour, then uncover and brush the tops of the potatoes with the remaining stock to moisten them. Cook for a further 45 minutes or until the meat and vegetables are very tender and the potato topping has browned.

Serve with: A green vegetable such as cabbage braised in the oven at the same time as the hotpot

Tips

★ Pack the vegetables and lamb as tightly as possible; the stock should barely cover the mixture – add a little more if necessary.

★ You can add other vegetables, if you like, such as turnips and halved button mushrooms.

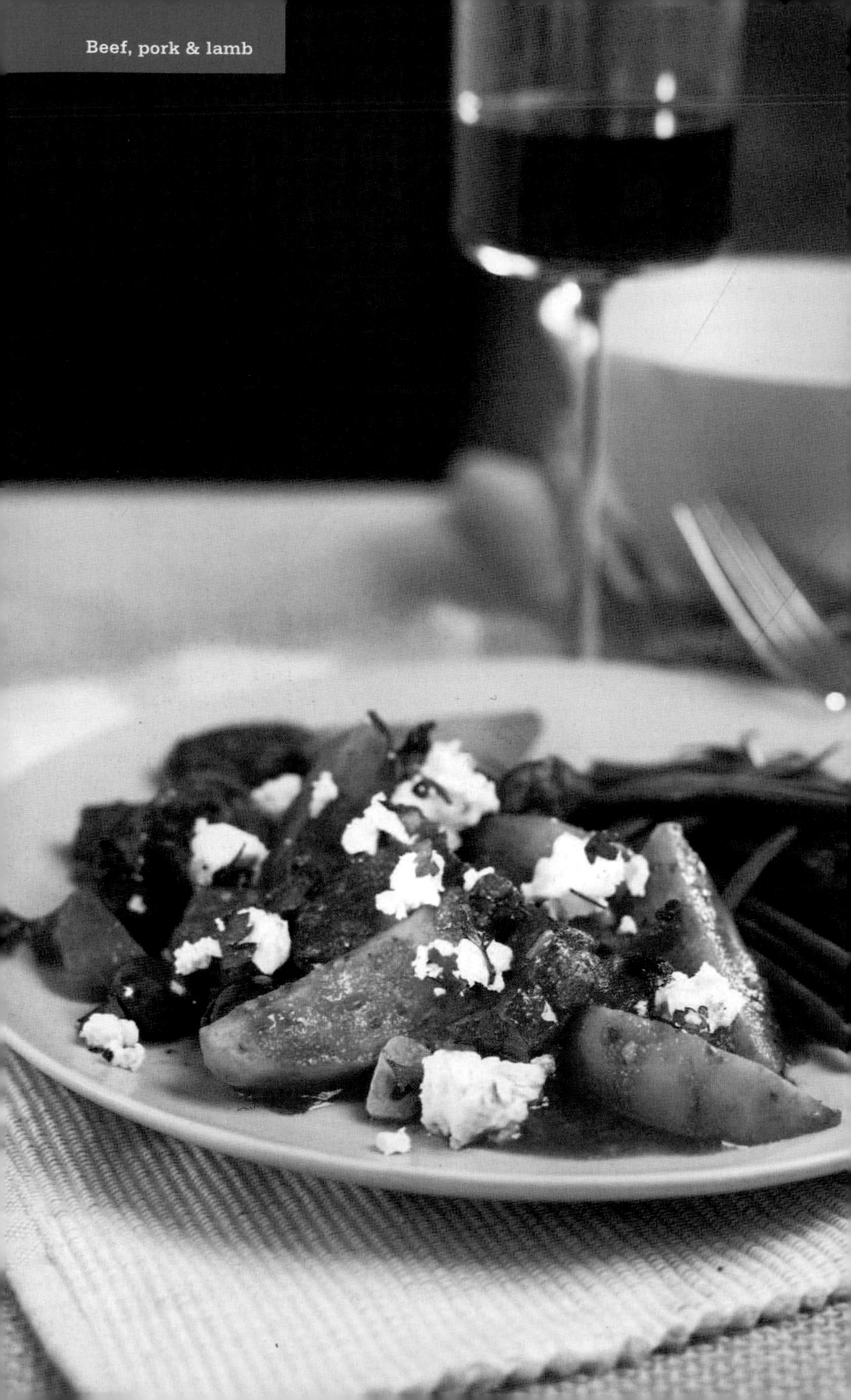

Greek lamb casserole

Serves 4
Ready in 2 hours

450 g/1 lb lamb neck fillet
10 ml/2 tsp olive oil
1 onion, thickly sliced
2 garlic cloves, chopped
300 ml/½ pint/1¼ cups lamb or vegetable stock
5 ml/1 tsp dried oregano
200 g/7 oz/small can of chopped tomatoes
Salt and freshly ground black pepper
450 g/1 lb small potatoes, peeled and cut into wedges
75 g/3 oz black olives, stoned (pitted)
75 g/3 oz Feta cheese, crumbled

1 Preheat the oven to 150°C/300°F/gas 2/fan oven 135°C. Trim any fat off the lamb and cut into 2 cm/¾ in cubes.

2 Heat the oil in a flameproof casserole dish (Dutch oven), add the meat and fry for 3–4 minutes until browned. Remove with a slotted spoon and transfer to a plate.

3 Add the onion and garlic and 45 ml/3 tbsp of the stock to the casserole and cook for 3–4 minutes or until all the stock has evaporated. Cook, stirring, for 1 minute or until the onions are just beginning to colour.

4 Return the meat and any juices to the casserole. Add the oregano, tomatoes and the remaining stock. Season with salt and pepper, stir, then slowly bring to the boil. Cover and cook in the oven for 45 minutes.

5 Add the potato wedges and olives to the casserole, re-cover and cook for a further 45 minutes or until the meat and potatoes are very tender. Taste and re-season, if necessary.

6 Ladle on to warm plates and scatter with the crumbled Feta just before serving.

Serve with: Boiled or steamed green beans

Tip

★ Feta cheese contains less fat than many cheeses. It is packed in brine, which gives it a very salty flavour, so be careful not to over-season this dish with salt.

Griddled lamb and pepper skewers with minted tomato couscous

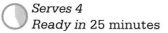
Serves 4
Ready in 25 minutes

3 large lamb steaks, each about 175 g/6 oz

10 ml/2 tsp olive oil

15 ml/1 tbsp fresh or bottled lemon juice

A large pinch of dried oregano

1 garlic clove, crushed

Salt and freshly ground black pepper

2 red (bell) peppers, halved, seeded and cut into squares

For the couscous:

250 g/9 oz/1½ cups couscous

450 ml/¾ pint/2 cups boiling vegetable stock

6 ripe tomatoes, roughly chopped

40 g/1½ oz walnut halves, roughly chopped

60 ml/4 tbsp chopped fresh mint leaves

Wedges of lemon to garnish (optional)

1 Cut out any bone and trim the fat off the lamb, then cut into 2 cm/¾ in cubes. Whisk together the oil, lemon juice, oregano, garlic and a little salt and pepper in a bowl. Add the lamb pieces and stir to coat in the marinade. Leave for 5 minutes, or cover and marinade in the fridge for several hours (or overnight if preferred).

2 Preheat the grill (broiler) to medium-high and line the grill pan with foil. Thread the lamb and peppers on to eight metal or soaked wooden skewers. Grill for 4–5 minutes on each side or until cooked to your liking.

3 Meanwhile, to make the couscous, place the couscous in a large bowl and pour the boiling stock over. Cover and leave for 7–8 minutes or until the couscous has absorbed all the liquid. Uncover and stir to separate the grains. Add the tomatoes, walnuts and mint to the couscous and stir in. Taste and season with a little salt and pepper, if necessary.

4 Serve the skewers on a bed of couscous, garnished with wedges of lemon.

Tip

★ You could thread other vegetables on to the skewers as well.

fish
&
seafood

Fish is the perfect food for our busy lives – quick and simple to cook and incredibly versatile. It makes a healthy choice for all kinds of meals as it is a great source of protein and provides many vitamins and minerals as well as being low in saturated fat. White fish contains less than 5 per cent fat, most of it polyunsaturated. 'Oily' fish contains between 5 and 15 per cent fat but these are the beneficial heart-healthy omega-3 fats that should be included in your diet. Although it was once advised that shellfish – especially prawns (shrimp) – should be avoided because of their cholesterol content, recent studies have shown that they are exceptionally low in saturated fat and that it is saturated fat which is the crucial risk factor for heart disease. The benefits from fish and shellfish mean they should be eaten at least twice a week.

Here you'll find wonderful fresh fish dishes such as Chilli-baked Plaice with Hot Onion Relish (see page 90) and Five-spice Trout and Stir-fried Vegetables (see page 98), as well as a selection of recipes using prepared seafood such as smoked salmon and convenient canned fish such as tuna. Special dishes, Seafood Paella, for instance (see page 89), are great for entertaining.

Seafood paella

 Serves 4
Ready in 30 minutes

10 ml/2 tsp olive oil

1 onion, thinly sliced

2 garlic cloves, crushed

900 ml/1½ pints/3¾ cups boiling fish or vegetable stock

1 red (bell) pepper, halved, seeded and sliced

2.5 ml/½ tsp ground paprika

A large pinch of saffron strands or ground turmeric

A large pinch of dried thyme or dried mixed herbs

225 g/8 oz/1 cup long-grain rice

200 g/7 oz/small can of chopped tomatoes

400 g/14 oz bag of mixed cooked seafood, thawed if frozen

1 lemon, cut into wedges (optional)

Salt and freshly ground black pepper

Flatleaf parsley leaves to garnish

1 Heat the oil in a large deep non-stick frying pan, add the onion and cook gently for 4–5 minutes. Add the garlic and 30 ml/2 tbsp of the stock and continue cooking until all the stock has evaporated. Stir in the pepper slices, the paprika, saffron or turmeric, herbs and rice. Cook, stirring, for a few seconds.

2 Add half of the remaining stock and the tomatoes. Stir the mixture and bring to the boil. Reduce the heat to low and simmer for 5 minutes or until almost all the liquid is absorbed.

3 Add the remaining stock and simmer for 10 minutes. Stir in the seafood and cook for a further 2–3 minutes or until the rice is tender and all the liquid has been absorbed. Season to taste with salt and pepper.

4 Remove the pan from the heat, cover and leave to stand for a minute or two. Spoon on to warm plates or deep bowls and serve with wedges of lemon, to squeeze over, if liked, and garnished with flatleaf parsley leaves.

Tip

★ You'll find mixed cooked seafood at the fish counter or in the frozen fish section. The contents may vary, but will usually be a combination of prawns (shrimp), mussels and squid rings. You can use a packet of cooked prawns if you prefer.

Chilli-baked plaice
with hot onion relish

Serves 4
Ready in 25 minutes

For the hot onion relish:

10 ml/2 tsp sunflower oil

45 ml/3 tbsp vegetable stock

1 large onion, thinly sliced

1 red chilli, seeded and finely chopped

30 ml/2 tbsp cider or white wine vinegar

10 ml/2 tsp light brown sugar

For the plaice:

6 plaice fillets, skinned

Salt and freshly ground black pepper

30 ml/2 tbsp sweet chilli sauce

30 ml/2 tbsp Thai fish sauce

30 ml/2 tbsp dry sherry, white wine or stock

Finely grated zest and juice of 1 lime

15 ml/1 tbsp light brown sugar

30 ml/2 tbsp chopped fresh coriander (cilantro)

1 red chilli, seeded and sliced

1   To make the relish, heat the oil and stock in a saucepan. Add the onion and chilli. Cover the pan with a lid and cook over a very low heat for 10 minutes, then remove the lid and simmer until all the stock has evaporated. Continue to cook, stirring frequently until the onion starts to colour, then add the vinegar and sugar, re-cover the pan and cook for 5 more minutes.

2   Meanwhile, preheat the oven to 200°C/400°F/gas 6/fan oven 180°C. Cut the plaice fillets in half lengthways and season lightly with salt and pepper. Turn the fillets so they are skinned-sides up, then roll up each one and place seam-side down in an ovenproof dish.

3   Mix together the remaining ingredients and spoon over the fish. Loosely cover the dish with foil and bake on the centre shelf of the oven for 15 minutes or until the fish is cooked through.

4   Divide the fish between four warm serving plates and spoon the cooking juices over. Serve the warm onion relish on the side.

Serve with: Steamed or boiled rice and sugar snap peas

Herb frittata
with smoked salmon

 Serves 4
Ready in 15 minutes

6 eggs

150 ml/¼ pint/⅔ cup skimmed milk

75 g/3 oz/¾ cup grated Emmenthal (Swiss) cheese

60 ml/4 tbsp chopped mixed fresh herbs such as parsley, chives and dill (dill weed)

Salt and freshly ground black pepper

5 ml/1 tsp butter, preferably unsalted (sweet), or sunflower margarine

150 g/5 oz thinly sliced smoked salmon

60 ml/4 tbsp half-fat crème fraîche or plain yoghurt

1 lemon, cut into wedges

1 Lightly beat the eggs in a bowl or jug with a fork. Add the milk, cheese, herbs and a little salt and pepper, then briefly whisk again.

2 Melt the butter or margarine in a large non-stick frying pan and swirl around the base. When hot, pour in the egg mixture and cook over a medium heat for 4–5 minutes until the frittata is golden-brown underneath.

3 Place the pan under a preheated hot grill (if your pan handle is wooden or plastic, cover it with foil) for 1–2 minutes until the top of the frittata is set and golden. Carefully remove from the pan and cut into eight wedges.

4 Arrange a wedge of frittata on each of four plates and top with a slice of smoked salmon. Repeat with a second wedge of frittata and slice of salmon. Add a spoonful of crème fraîche and a wedge of lemon to squeeze over the salmon.

Serve with: A mixed baby leaf salad

Tips

★ Use 5 ml/1 tsp of olive or sunflower oil to fry the frittata, if preferred.

★ Smoked salmon is already lightly salted, so take care when seasoning the egg mixture.

★ Choose very thinly sliced smoked salmon for this recipe, either cold-smoked or hot-smoked (which has a slightly smoky, roasted flavour). You could also use gravid lax (marinated salmon with dill) and reduce the amount of herbs in the frittata.

Potato-topped cod
with green herb dressing

Serves 4
Ready in 25 minutes

350 g/12 oz small new potatoes, scrubbed

30 ml/2 tbsp low-fat spread or sunflower margarine

Salt and freshly ground black pepper

4 cod loin fillets, about 200 g/7 oz each

15 ml/1 tbsp lemon juice

For the dressing:

10 ml/2 tsp Dijon mustard

60 ml/4 tbsp reduced-fat mayonnaise

4 cornichons (baby gherkins), finely chopped

60 ml/4 tbsp chopped fresh herbs such as parsley, chives, tarragon and basil

1 Bring a pan of water to the boil, add the potatoes and bring back to the boil. Reduce the heat, half-cover the pan with a lid and simmer for 5 minutes. Drain the potatoes and rinse briefly under cold water so that they are still warm but are cool enough to handle.

2 Slice the potatoes very thinly and place in a bowl with the low-fat spread or margarine. Season with salt and pepper and toss together gently until the spread or margarine has melted and lightly coated the potato slices.

3 Place the cod on a grill (broiler) pan lined with foil and sprinkle with half the lemon juice. Arrange the potato slices over the fish in overlapping rows. Cook the potato-topped cod under a preheated medium-high grill for 8–10 minutes or until the potatoes are tender and lightly browned and the fish flakes easily and is just cooked through.

4 Meanwhile, to make the dressing, whisk together the remaining lemon juice with the mustard and mayonnaise. Stir in the cornichons and herbs, then season to taste with salt and pepper.

5 Place the fish on warm serving plates and serve with a large spoonful of the dressing alongside.

Serve with: Wedges of lemon, roasted squash and mangetout (snow peas)

Tip

★ Pieces of hake, halibut, hoki or salmon can be used instead of cod.

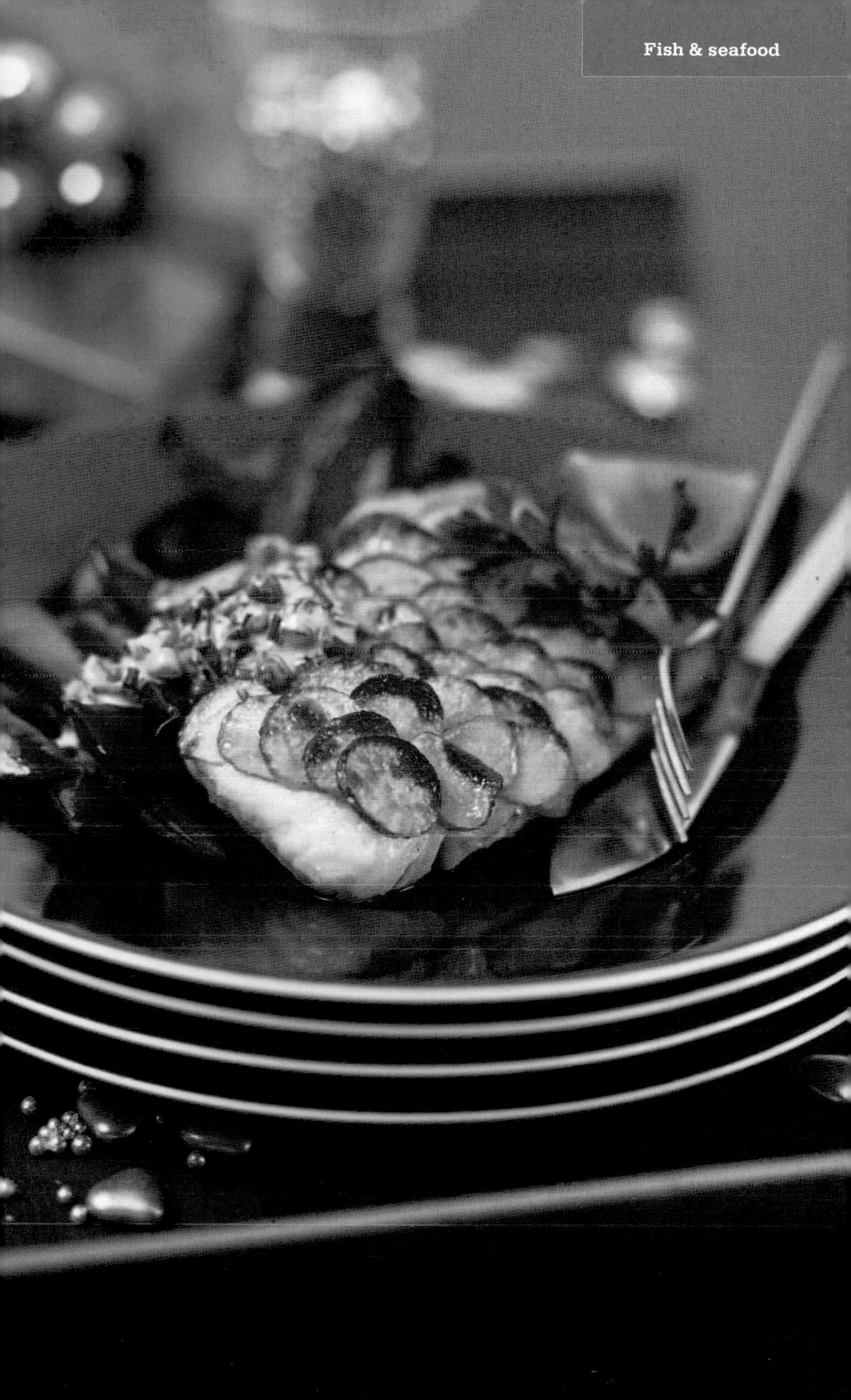

Seafood salad

Serves 4
Ready in 20 minutes

8 small squid, cleaned and sliced
100 g/4 oz stir-fry rice noodles
45 ml/3 tbsp Thai fish sauce
Finely grated zest and juice of 2 limes
1 red chilli, seeded and finely chopped
5 ml/1 tsp light brown sugar
10 ml/2 tsp rice, sherry or cider vinegar
12 cooked and peeled tiger prawns (shrimp)
1 small ripe avocado, peeled and sliced
A small bunch of mint leaves
100 g/4 oz mixed salad leaves
1 orange, peeled and segmented
Salt and freshly ground black pepper

1 Pour about 2.5 cm/1 in of water into a large saucepan. Bring to the boil, add the squid and cook for 2–3 minutes or until just cooked and tender. Remove with a slotted spoon and leave on a plate to cool.

2 Pour more boiling water into the saucepan so it is about half-full. Bring back to the boil, then add the noodles and cook for 3 minutes or according to the packet instructions until tender. Drain well, then tip into a bowl of cold water until ready to use.

3 Mix together the fish sauce, lime zest and juice, the chilli, sugar and vinegar. Add the squid, prawns and avocado slices and stir to lightly coat in the dressing.

4 Reserve a few sprigs of mint for garnish and chop the remainder. Drain the noodles and cut into 10 cm/4 in pieces. Mix with the chopped mint and salad leaves, then pile on to four plates. Top with the squid, prawns, avocado slices and orange segments.

5 Spoon over any dressing left in the bowl and serve garnished with mint sprigs.

Tips

★ If preferred, use a 400 g/14 oz bag of mixed seafood instead of the squid and tiger prawns.

★ You could use vegetable stock instead of water for added flavour.

Five-spice trout
and stir-fried vegetables

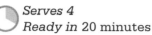
Serves 4
Ready in 20 minutes

10 ml/2 tsp toasted sesame oil

400 g/14 oz fine green beans, trimmed

1 bunch of spring onions (scallions), trimmed and cut into thirds

225 g/8 oz shiitake mushrooms, halved

10 ml/2 tsp fresh or bottled grated root ginger

90 ml/6 tbsp vegetable stock

5 ml/1 tsp Chinese five-spice powder

4 trout fillets

10 ml/2 tsp sunflower oil

100 ml/3½ fl oz/scant ½ cup oyster sauce

Salt and freshly ground black pepper

1 Heat the sesame oil in a large non-stick frying pan or wok. Add the beans, spring onions and mushrooms and cook for 2 minutes, stirring all the time.

2 Add the ginger and stock, cover the pan with a lid and cook for a further 3 minutes until tender.

3 Meanwhile, sprinkle the five-spice powder on the trout fillets. Heat the sunflower oil in a non-stick frying pan, add the trout fillets, flesh-side down, and cook for 3 minutes. Turn over and cook for 3 more minutes or until the fish is cooked through and just flakes.

4 Stir the oyster sauce into the vegetables and season to taste with salt and pepper. Divide the vegetables between four warm serving plates and place the trout fillets on top.

Serve with: Steamed or boiled rice noodles

Tips

★ Oyster sauce is a thick brown Chinese condiment, traditionally made from just oysters, but now more likely to be flavoured with oyster extract.

★ Like other oily fish, trout contains beneficial fats from the omega-3 family of essential fatty acids, which help to protect the body against heart disease.

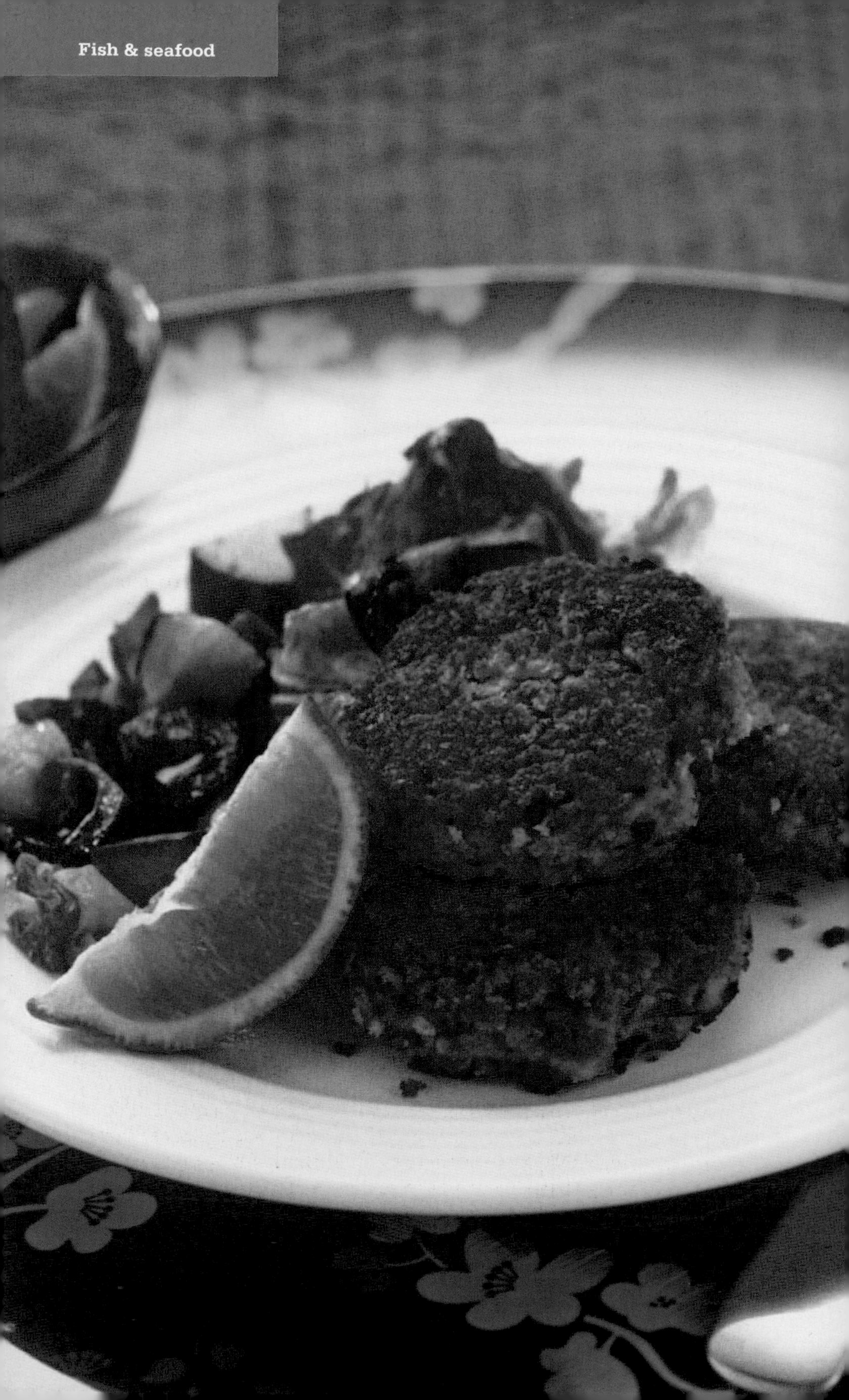

Tasty tuna fishcakes

 Serves 4
Ready in 45 minutes

400 g/14 oz potatoes, peeled and cubed

30 ml/2 tbsp skimmed milk

30 ml/2 tbsp reduced-fat pesto

Finely grated zest of ½ lemon

Salt and freshly ground black pepper

2 x 200 g/7 oz/small cans of tuna, drained

25 g/1 oz/¼ cup plain (all-purpose) flour

1 egg

75 g/3 oz/1½ cups fresh wholemeal or white breadcrumbs

20 g/¾ oz/3 tbsp Parmesan cheese, finely grated

1 Cook the potatoes in lightly salted boiling water for 15 minutes or until tender. Drain and mash with the milk, pesto and lemon zest. Season to taste with salt and pepper and leave to cool.

2 Roughly break up the tuna into chunks and stir into the potatoes. Shape the mixture into eight thick, flat cakes and dust on both sides with flour.

3 Lightly beat the egg on a plate with a fork and combine the breadcrumbs and Parmesan on another plate. Coat the fishcakes first in the egg, then in the crumbs. Chill until ready to cook.

4 Preheat the oven to 190°C/375°F/gas 5/fan oven 170°C. Place the fishcakes on a non-stick baking (cookie) sheet and bake in the oven for 15 minutes or until golden-brown and hot in the middle.

Serve with: A mixed green salad and wedges of lemon

Tips

* For very low-fat fishcakes, use tuna in spring water or brine.

* Instead of canned tuna, you could use fresh fish in these fishcakes. Put 400 g/14 oz of white fish fillets such as haddock in a saucepan and pour over just enough milk, stock or water to cover. Bring almost to boiling, then lower the heat, cover and poach gently for 5 minutes or until it will flake easily. Remove the fish and flake, discarding any skin and bones.

* Adding a little Parmesan to the coating not only adds flavour but also helps give the fishcakes a deep golden-brown colour when baked.

Smoked salmon tagliatelle

Serves 4
Ready in 20 minutes

350 g/12 oz tagliatelle
150 g/5 oz extra-light soft cheese
Finely grated zest of 1 lemon
15 ml/1 tbsp lemon juice
15 ml/1 tbsp chopped fresh dill (dill weed)
150 g/5 oz smoked salmon, cut into thin strips
Salt and freshly ground black pepper
Black lumpfish roe to serve (optional)

1 Cook the tagliatelle in lightly salted boiling water for 10 minutes or according to the packet instructions. When the pasta is al dente (tender but still firm to the bite), drain well in a colander, reserving the cooking liquid in a jug.

2 Put the cheese in a small pan with the lemon zest and juice and 100 ml/ 3½ fl oz/scant ½ cup of the cooking liquid. Heat gently until the mixture is steaming hot, stirring until the cheese has melted and makes a thick creamy sauce.

3 Stir the dill and smoked salmon into the sauce and season with salt and pepper to taste.

4 Return the tagliatelle to the large pan, pour the sauce over and gently mix everything together. Divide the pasta between four warm plates and serve each with a spoonful of black lumpfish roe, if liked.

Tips

★ Recipes often recommend adding a spoonful of oil to the pan when cooking pasta to stop it sticking together, which isn't necessary if you are serving the pasta with a sauce. To keep the pasta pieces separate, always use plenty of boiling water, pour in the pasta, then give it a stir and bring back to the boil. Turn down the heat just a little until the water is still boiling but not too fiercely.

★ For a low-fat tomato sauce for pasta, gently cook 1 finely chopped garlic clove and 1 seeded and finely chopped red chilli in 5 ml/1 tsp of olive oil. Add a 400 g/14 oz/large can of chopped tomatoes with basil or (bell) peppers and simmer uncovered for about 10 minutes until thick. Add the pasta and toss together. Serve scattered with a little freshly grated Parmesan cheese.

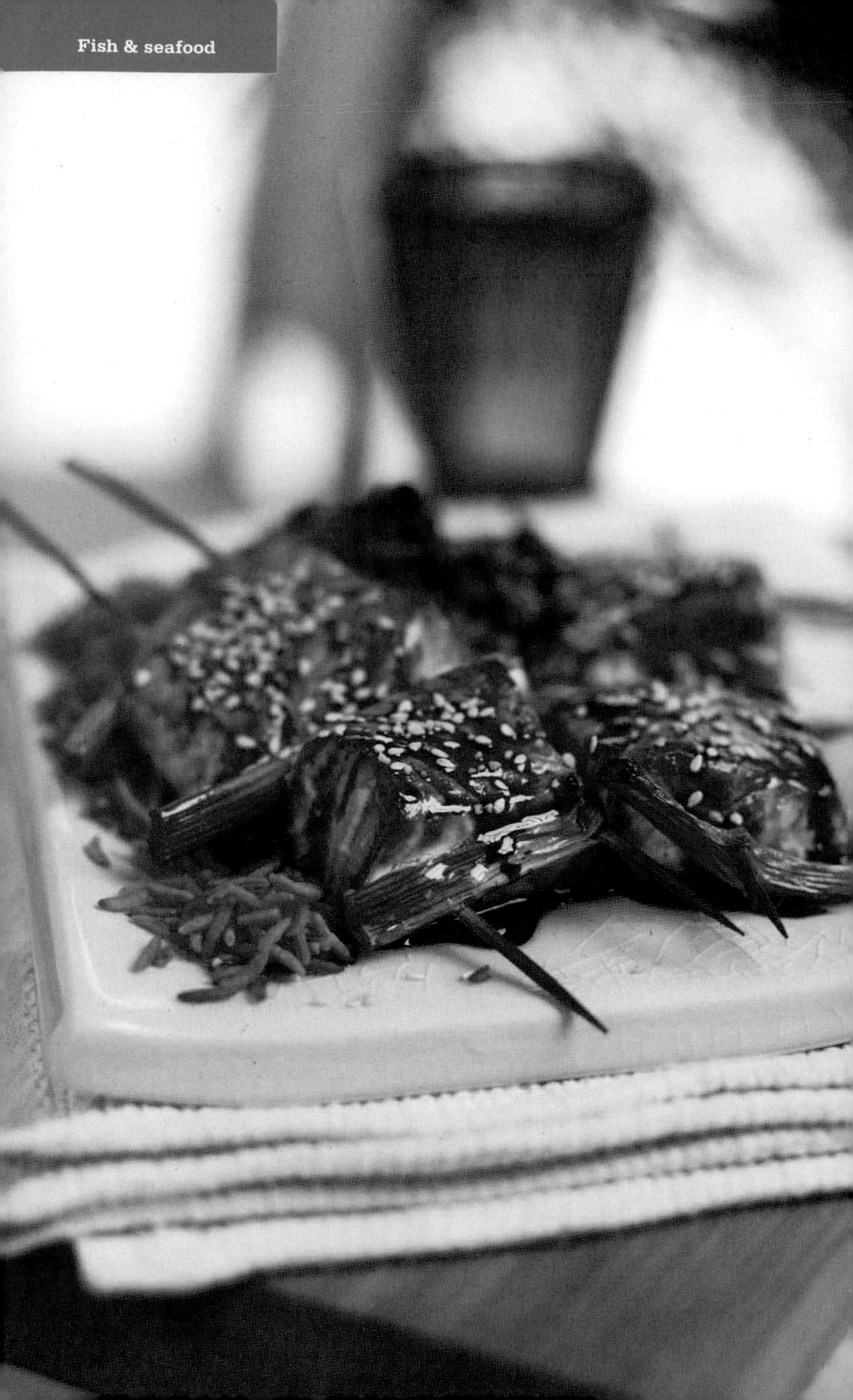

Salmon teriyaki skewers
with lemon rice

Serves 4
Ready in 30 minutes

600 g/1 lb 6 oz thick salmon fillets, skinned

30 ml/2 tbsp Japanese soy sauce

30 ml/2 tbsp mirin or medium sherry

1 garlic clove, very finely chopped

15 ml/1 tbsp fresh or bottled grated root ginger

5 ml/1 tsp light brown sugar

8 spring onions (scallions), trimmed

15 ml/1 tbsp sesame seeds

For the lemon rice:

300 g/11 oz long-grain white rice, rinsed

A pinch of saffron strands or ground turmeric

A strip of lemon zest

1 litre/1¾ pints/4¼ cups boiling vegetable stock

15 ml/1 tbsp lemon juice

Salt and freshly ground black pepper

1 Cut the salmon into 16 bite-sized chunks. Put the soy sauce, mirin or sherry, garlic, ginger and sugar in a mixing bowl and whisk together. Add the salmon to the mixture and turn so that the pieces are thoroughly coated. Cover and leave to marinate for 10 minutes.

2 Meanwhile, start to cook the lemon rice. Put the rice in a pan with the saffron or turmeric and lemon zest. Add the stock and bring to the boil. Stir, then cover and simmer gently for 10–15 minutes or until the rice is tender and has absorbed all the liquid.

3 Cut the spring onions into 6 cm/2½ in lengths. Thread the salmon pieces and spring onion pieces alternately on to soaked wooden skewers.

4 Preheat the grill (broiler) to moderately hot and line the grill pan with foil. Grill (broil) the skewers for 2–3 minutes on each side, brushing with any remaining marinade, until the fish is just cooked through and opaque. Sprinkle the sesame seeds over for the last 30 seconds of grilling time.

5 Stir the lemon juice into the rice, taste and season with salt and pepper. Spoon on to warm plates and top with the salmon skewers.

Serve with: Steamed peas

vegetables

&

vegetarian

Being a vegetarian doesn't mean sitting down to only bland and monotonous meals – just as being a meat-eater doesn't mean you can't cook and enjoy these meat-free meals. Here you'll find recipes that make use of all kinds of naturally low-fat ingredients from vegetables, beans and pulses to grains and pasta.

It's important that vegetarians trying to follow a low-fat diet don't rely too heavily on cheese as a protein ingredient as about one-third of hard cheese such as Cheddar is saturated fat. There's no need to cut it out completely, though, and it's a useful source of protein for vegetarians, but do try the reduced-fat versions or use a mature or strongly flavoured variety, which will add lots of taste to your food in just a small amount. Use naturally lower-fat cheeses as well in cooking, like Feta and Ricotta.

Foods such as avocados, seeds and nuts are moderately high in fat, but these are healthy monounsaturated fats and should be included in your diet – as always, moderation and common sense are the key.

Roasted butternut squash
with blue cheese and sage

Serves 4
Ready in 45 minutes

2 butternut squashes

10 ml/2 tsp olive oil

15 ml/1 tbsp water

1 small onion, finely chopped

2 garlic cloves, crushed

2 leeks, shredded

1 red chilli, seeded and finely chopped, or 2.5 ml/½ tsp chilli powder

A small handful of fresh sage leaves

Salt and freshly ground black pepper

100 g/4 oz blue cheese such as Stilton or Gorgonzola, crumbled

1 Preheat the oven to 200°C/400°F/gas 6/fan oven 180°C. Halve the squashes lengthwise and scoop out the seeds. Place cut-side up in a roasting tin, cover with foil and bake for 10 minutes or until starting to soften.

2 Scoop the flesh out of the squashes, taking care not to damage the outer skin, and chop it into small cubes.

3 Heat the oil and water in a non-stick frying pan. Add the onion, garlic and leeks, cover with a lid and cook for 5 minutes.

4 Uncover the pan, add the squash and chilli and cook for a further 5 minutes, stirring occasionally, until all the liquid has evaporated.

5 Reserve a few sage leaves for garnishing and roughly chop the rest. Stir the chopped sage into the vegetable mixture and season with salt and pepper. Pile the mixture into the squash shells and sprinkle the cheese over the tops.

6 Bake uncovered for 20 minutes until the cheese is melted and bubbling and the vegetable filling is tender. Garnish each with fresh sage leaves before serving.

Tip

★ To make a dish suitable for vegans, leave out the blue cheese and sprinkle the tops with a mixture of 50 g/2 oz/1 cup of fresh white or wholemeal breadcrumbs and 15 ml/1 tbsp each of pumpkin and sunflower seeds.

Vegetarian shepherd's pie

Serves 4
Ready in 30 minutes

750 g/1¾ lb mixed root vegetables such as carrots, swede (rutabaga) and parsnips, peeled and diced

30 ml/2 tbsp skimmed milk

Salt and freshly ground black pepper

5 ml/1 tsp olive oil

1 red onion, finely chopped

15 ml/1 tbsp vegetable stock or water

400 g/14 oz/large can of chopped tomatoes with chilli

250 ml/8 fl oz/1 cup passata (sieved tomatoes)

2.5 ml/½ tsp dried mixed herbs

300 g/11 oz fresh or frozen minced (ground) Quorn

5 ml/1 tsp cornflour (cornstarch)

10 ml/2 tsp dark soy sauce

75 g/3 oz/¾ cup frozen peas

1 Cook the diced vegetables in a pan of lightly salted boiling water for 10–12 minutes or until just tender. Drain well, return to the pan and mash well. Add the milk and a little salt and pepper, then beat well until smooth and creamy. Cover the pan with a lid to keep the mash warm.

2 Meanwhile, heat the oil in a non-stick frying pan and add the onion and stock or water. Cook, stirring frequently, until the liquid has evaporated, then add the tomatoes, passata, herbs and Quorn. Bring to the boil, then simmer for 5 minutes until the sauce has reduced a little.

3 Mix the cornflour and soy sauce to a paste and stir into the Quorn mixture with the peas. Bring back to the boil, stirring until thickened. Season with salt and pepper.

4 Preheat the grill to medium. Spoon the Quorn mixture into a heatproof dish and top with the mashed vegetables. Using a fork, rough up the top, then grind over a little black pepper. Grill for 4–5 minutes or until the top is lightly browned.

Serve with: **Fresh vegetables such as beans, sweetcorn and carrots**

Tip

★ Quorn is very low in fat and calories, yet high in fibre and protein, so it's a great source of complete protein for vegetarians. However, it's unsuitable for vegans because it contains egg albumen.

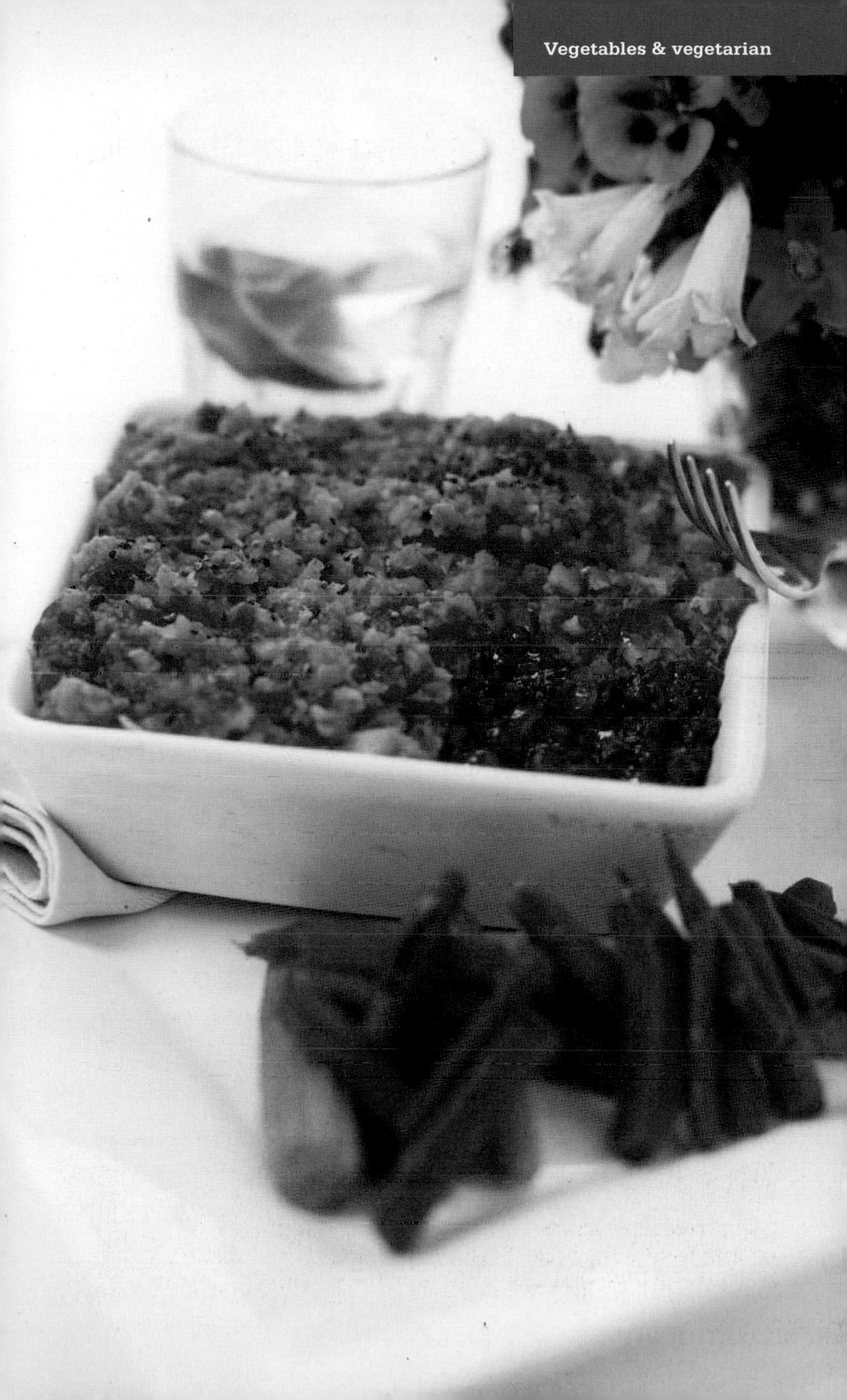

Herby polenta and mushrooms

Serves 4
Ready in 45 minutes

15 g/½ oz/1 tbsp sunflower margarine

750 ml/1¼ pints/3 cups vegetable stock

½ small Savoy cabbage, finely shredded

1 red (bell) pepper, seeded and finely diced

75 g/3 oz quick-cook polenta

30 ml/2 tbsp chopped fresh parsley or chives, plus extra to garnish

1 egg yolk

Salt and freshly ground black pepper

5 ml/1 tsp olive oil, plus extra for greasing

50 g/2 oz Emmenthal (Swiss) cheese, finely grated

450 g/1lb mixed mushrooms such as chestnut, oyster and shiitake

30 ml/2 tbsp sweet sherry

150 ml/¼ pint/⅔ cup half-fat crème fraîche

1 Heat the margarine and 60 ml/4 tbsp of the stock in a frying pan. Add the cabbage and diced pepper and stir well. Cover and cook for 5 minutes. Remove the lid and continue to cook, stirring occasionally, until the vegetables are tender and the liquid has evaporated. Set aside.

2 Meanwhile, preheat the oven to 200°C/400°F/gas 6/fan oven 180°C. Pour the remaining stock into a saucepan and bring to the boil. Add the polenta in a steady stream, stirring all the time, and cook for about 5 minutes or according to the packet instructions.

3 Stir the vegetable mixture, herbs and egg yolk into the polenta and season. Transfer the mixture to a lightly greased 20 cm/8 in loose-bottomed or springform round tin and smooth the surface level. Sprinkle the cheese over the top and bake for 15 minutes until golden-brown.

4 While the polenta is baking, heat the oil and 15 ml/1 tbsp of water in the frying pan. Add the mushrooms and stir-fry for 5 minutes over a moderately high heat. Add the sherry and cook for a further 2–3 minutes or until all the liquid has evaporated.

5 Add the crème fraîche and heat gently until piping hot but do not boil or the crème fraîche may separate. Season with salt and pepper.

6 Carefully remove the baked polenta from the tin and cut it into four wedges. Place on warm serving plates, then spoon the mushroom sauce over and garnish with chopped parsley or chives.

Turkish stuffed aubergines

Serves 4
Ready in 45 minutes

75 g/3 oz/½ cup raisins

4 aubergines (eggplants), each about 250 g/9 oz

Finely grated zest and juice of 1 lemon

Salt and freshly ground black pepper

10 ml/2 tsp olive oil

75 ml/5 tbsp vegetable stock

2 onions, finely chopped

2 garlic cloves, crushed

8 tomatoes, skinned, seeded and chopped

A pinch of cayenne pepper

5 ml/1 tsp chopped fresh thyme

4 bay leaves

1 Preheat the oven to 200°C/400°F/gas 6/fan oven 180°C. Put the raisins in a small bowl and pour over enough warm water to cover. Leave to soak.

2 Cut the aubergines in half lengthways and score the cut sides deeply without damaging the skins. Place, scored-side, up in an ovenproof dish. Rub in some of the lemon juice and sprinkle with a little salt. Bake for 20 minutes until soft and tender.

3 Carefully scoop out the flesh from the aubergines to leave the skins intact and chop the flesh finely.

4 Heat the oil and 30 ml/2 tbsp of the stock in a frying pan, add the onions and cook for 5–7 minutes, stirring frequently, until all the stock has evaporated, then cook for a further minute or two, stirring all the time, until the onions begin to colour.

5 Stir in the garlic, chopped aubergines, tomatoes, cayenne pepper, thyme, lemon zest and the remaining stock. Cook gently for 5 minutes or until most of the stock has evaporated. Season with salt and pepper.

6 Place the hollowed-out aubergine skins in the ovenproof dish. Fill them with the vegetable mixture and lay the bay leaves on top, then cook in the oven for 15 minutes. Sprinkle with the lemon juice before serving.

Serve with: Warmed flatbreads or pittas

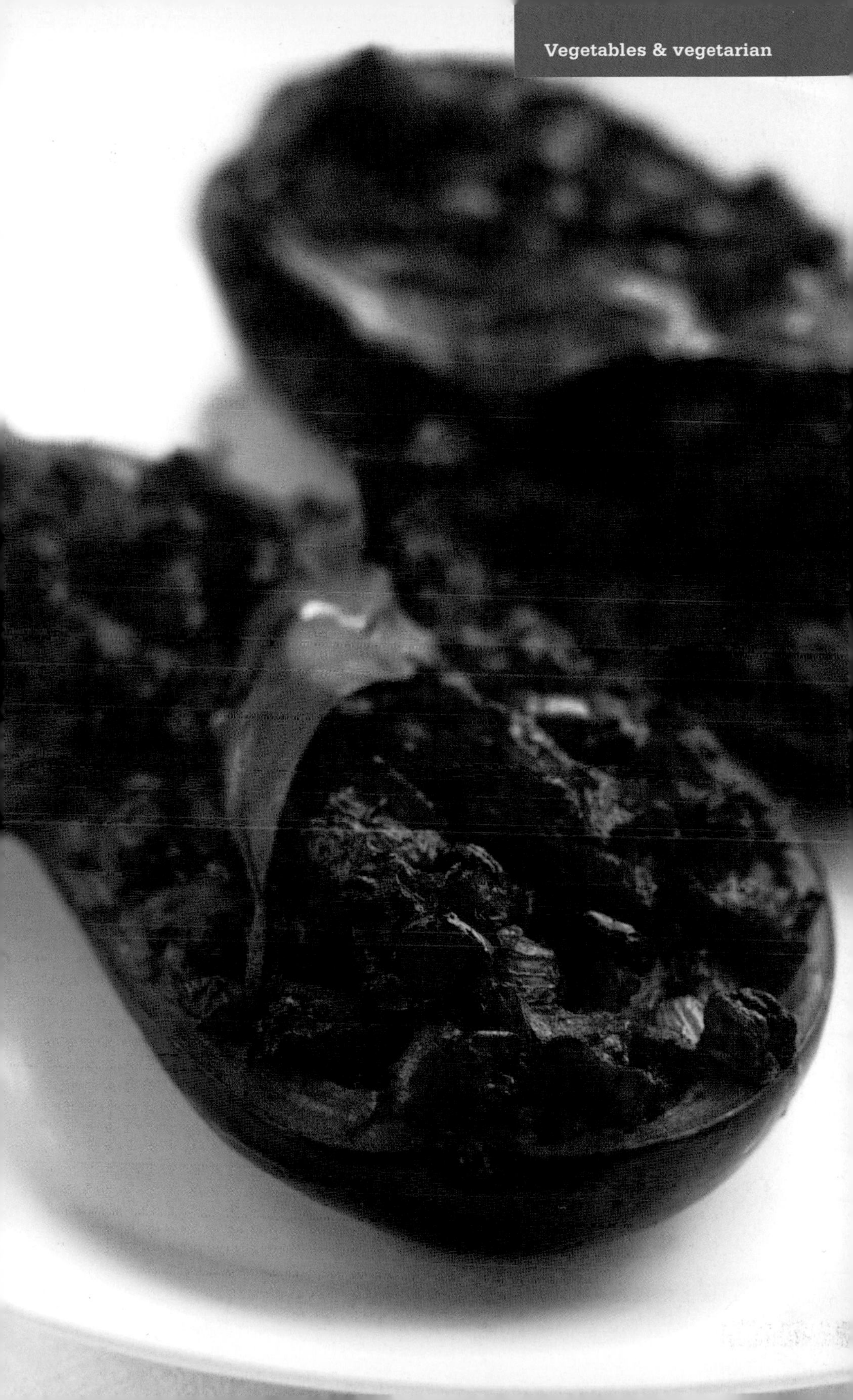

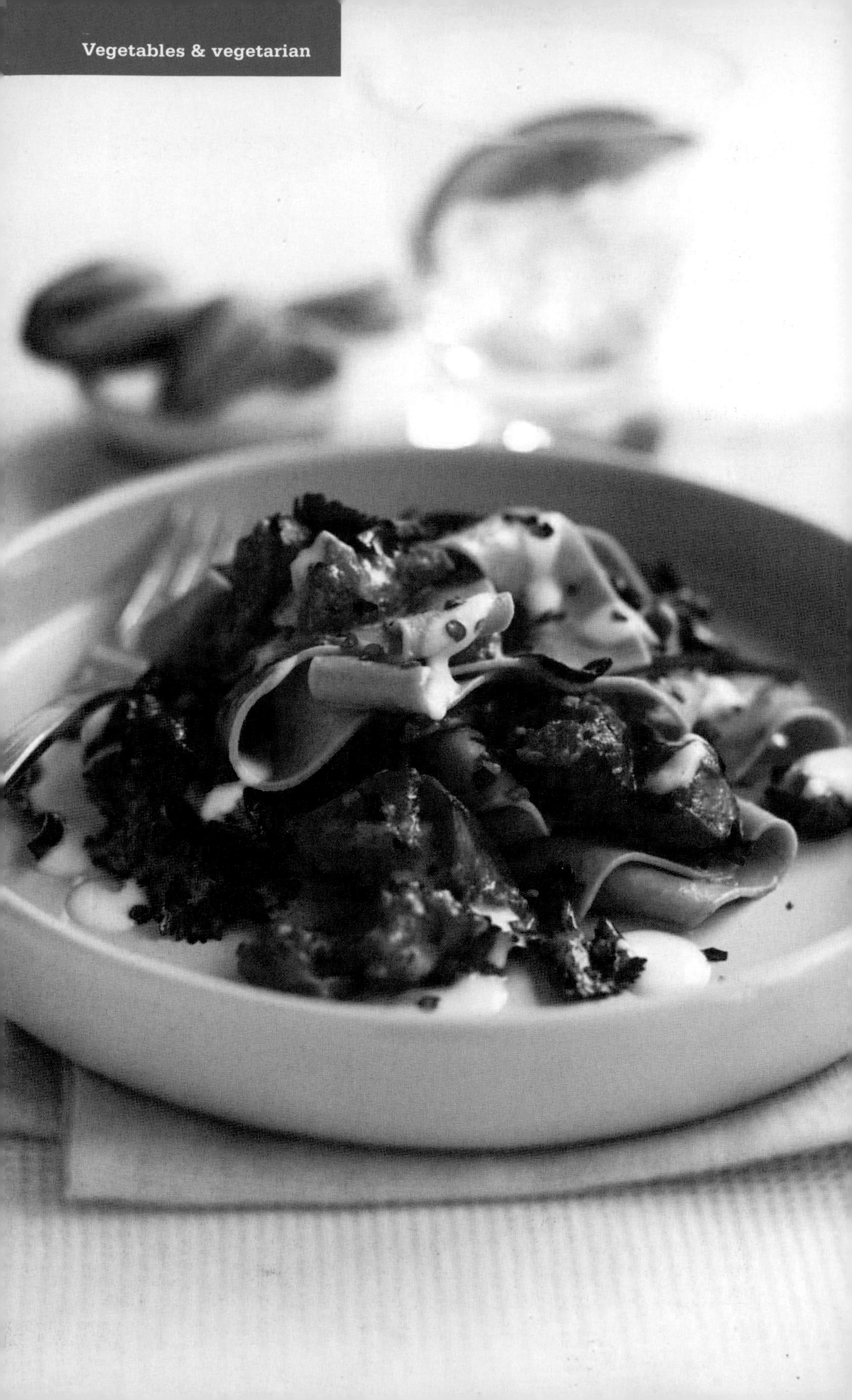

Sweet potato and spinach
pasta

Serves 4
Ready in 30 minutes

350 g/12 oz sweet potatoes, peeled and diced

1 garlic clove, crushed

10 ml/2 tsp olive oil

Salt and freshly ground black pepper

350 g/12 oz pappardelle

225 g/8 oz baby spinach leaves

75 ml/5 tbsp reduced-fat coconut milk

5 ml/1 tsp dried chilli flakes

Leaves from a small bunch of fresh coriander (cilantro)

1 Preheat the oven to 190°C/375°F/gas 5/fan oven 170°C. Put the sweet potatoes and garlic in a bowl and drizzle with the olive oil. Season with salt and pepper. Mix together with your hands so that the potato pieces are lightly covered in oil. Spread the sweet potato in a single layer in a roasting tin and bake for 20 minutes or until tender.

2 Meanwhile, cook the pappardelle in a large pan of lightly salted boiling water for 10 minutes or according to the packet instructions. Drain thoroughly.

3 When the sweet potato is cooked, transfer the roasting tin to the hob, add the spinach and cook over a gentle heat for 2–3 minutes until just wilted. Stir in the coconut milk and chilli flakes.

4 Add the pasta and coriander leaves and mix together over a very low heat. Taste and adjust the seasoning, if necessary. Divide between four warm plates and serve straight away.

Tips

★ Pappardelle are broad noodles, usually 2–3 cm/¾–1¼ in wide. If you prefer, use thinner noodles such as tagliatelle or fettucine.

★ Instead of sweet potatoes, try roasting a medium-sized aubergine (eggplant) and courgette (zucchini), both diced and tossed in a little olive oil as before. Instead of coconut milk, use 150 ml/¼ pint/⅔ cup of passata (sieved tomatoes).

Speedy vegetable stir-fry

 Serves 4
Ready in 20 minutes

10 ml/2 tsp sesame oil

10 ml/2 tsp fresh or bottled grated root ginger

1 red chilli, seeded and cut into thin strips

1 yellow (bell) pepper, halved, seeded and cut into strips

1 large carrot, sliced

175 g/6 oz broccoli florets

175 g/6 oz mangetout (snow peas)

60 ml/4 tbsp vegetable stock or water

1 garlic clove, finely chopped

200 g/7 oz/small can of water chestnuts, drained and sliced

200 g/7 oz mung bean or medium egg noodles

45 ml/3 tbsp light soy sauce

20 ml/1½ tbsp toasted sesame seeds

1 Heat the sesame oil in a large non-stick frying pan or wok. Add the ginger and chilli and stir-fry for 1 minute.

2 Add the pepper strips, carrot, broccoli, mangetout and stock or water. Cook over a high heat, stirring all the time, for 5–8 minutes or until tender. Stir in the garlic and water chestnuts and cook for a further minute.

3 Meanwhile, cook the noodles in boiling water, allowing 5 minutes for mung bean noodles and 4 minutes for egg noodles or according to the packet instructions. Drain well.

4 Add the noodles to the vegetables with the soy sauce and toss well to mix everything together. Sprinkle with the sesame seeds and serve straight away in warm shallow bowls or plates.

Tips

★ Some supermarkets sell ready-toasted sesame seeds. Alternatively, toast sesame seeds before stir-frying the vegetables in the dry frying pan or wok over a medium heat until golden, stirring all the time.

★ Use your favourite vegetables in this stir-fry: baby sweetcorn, trimmed and halved fine green beans, oyster or baby button mushrooms and sliced spring onions (scallions) would all work well.

★ For an even faster stir-fry, use two 150 g/5 oz packets of straight-to-wok noodles and a large packet of ready-prepared stir-fry vegetables.

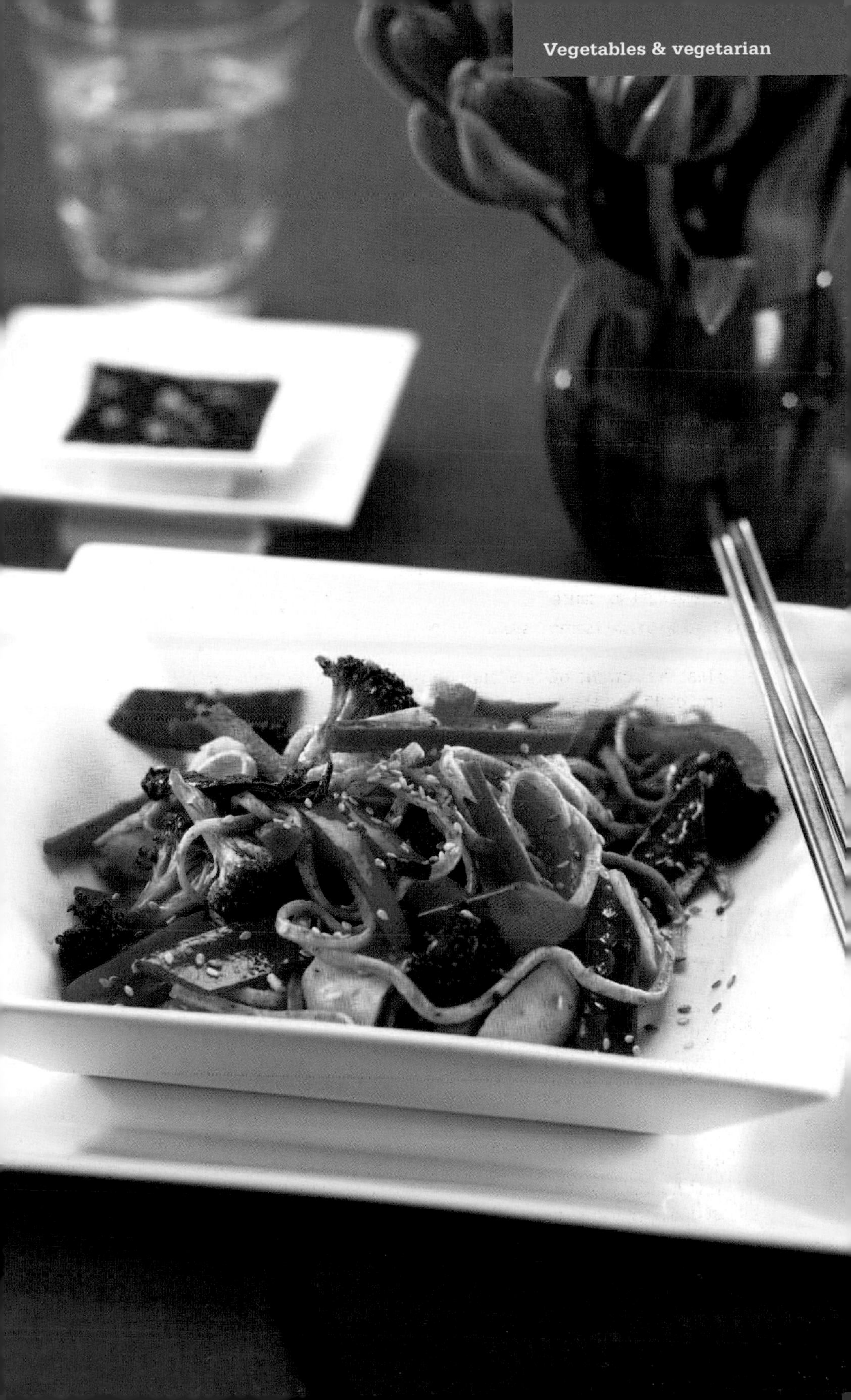

Caribbean-style ratatouille

Serves 4
Ready in 45 minutes

175 g/6 oz sweet potato, peeled

175 g/6 oz butternut squash, peeled and seeded

1 aubergine (eggplant), about 250 g/9 oz

1 red (bell) pepper, halved and seeded

1 onion, peeled and sliced

15 ml/1 tbsp olive oil

15 ml/1 tbsp vegetable stock or water

2 garlic cloves, crushed

2 courgettes (zucchini), sliced

A pinch of dried chilli flakes

15 ml/1 tbsp chopped fresh thyme

400 g/14 oz/large can of chopped tomatoes

200 ml/7 fl oz/scant 1 cup passata (sieved tomatoes)

Salt and freshly ground black pepper

15 ml/1 tbsp chopped fresh parsley

1 Preheat the oven to 220°C/425°F/gas 7/fan oven 200°C. Cut the sweet potato, squash, aubergine and red pepper into 2.5 cm/1 in cubes. Place in a non-stick roasting tin with the onion and drizzle the oil and stock or water over. Toss the vegetables with your hands to coat and cook in the oven for 15 minutes.

2 Remove the vegetables from the oven and turn them. Add the garlic and courgettes and cook in the oven for a further 10 minutes or until the vegetables are just tender.

3 Stir together the chilli flakes, thyme, tomatoes and passata and season with salt and pepper. Pour over the vegetables, mix everything together, then return to the oven and cook for a further 15 minutes. Scatter with the fresh parsley to garnish and serve.

Serve with: Steamed or boiled rice

Tip

★ Check the vegetables occasionally while they are roasting. If some pieces are browning quite quickly, turn them over so that everything browns evenly.

Nut loaf with tomato sauce

Serves 4
Ready in 1 hour

10 ml/2 tsp olive oil
30 ml/2 tbsp vegetable stock
1 onion, finely chopped
1 leek, finely chopped
225 g/8 oz mushrooms, chopped
2 garlic cloves, crushed
25 g/1 oz/¼ cup plain (all-purpose) flour
400 g/14 oz/large can of lentils, rinsed and drained
75 g/3 oz/¾ cup mixed nuts such as hazelnuts (filberts), brazils and almonds, finely chopped
50 g/2 oz/½ cup grated mature Cheddar cheese
1 egg, lightly beaten
60 ml/4 tbsp chopped fresh mixed herbs
Salt and freshly ground black pepper
For the tomato-pepper sauce:
1 red (bell) pepper, finely diced
400 g/14 oz/large can of chopped tomatoes with herbs

1 Preheat the oven to 190°C/375°F/gas 5/fan oven 170°C. Line the base and sides of a 900 g/2 lb loaf tin with non-stick baking parchment. Heat the oil and stock in a large saucepan. Add the onion and leek, stir well, then cover with a lid and cook over a medium heat for 5 minutes.

2 Remove the lid and spoon about a third of the onion and leek mixture into a small bowl. Add the mushrooms and garlic to the rest of the mixture in the pan and cook for a further 5 minutes until the vegetables are soft, stirring occasionally. Turn up the heat a little and cook until all the liquid has evaporated and the onions are browning. Turn off the heat.

3 Sprinkle the flour over the mixture and stir in. Add the lentils, nuts, cheese, egg and herbs and season well. Mix together thoroughly. Spoon the mixture into the prepared loaf tin, pressing it into the corners, then level the surface. Bake, uncovered, for 40–45 minutes or until lightly browned and firm to the touch. Leave to stand in the tin for 5 minutes.

4 While the loaf is cooking, put all the sauce ingredients in a small saucepan with the reserved onion and leek mixture. Simmer uncovered for 7–8 minutes or until the sauce has thickened slightly and the vegetables are tender. Cut the loaf into thick slices and serve with the sauce.

Serve with: Broccoli, cauliflower and sauté potatoes

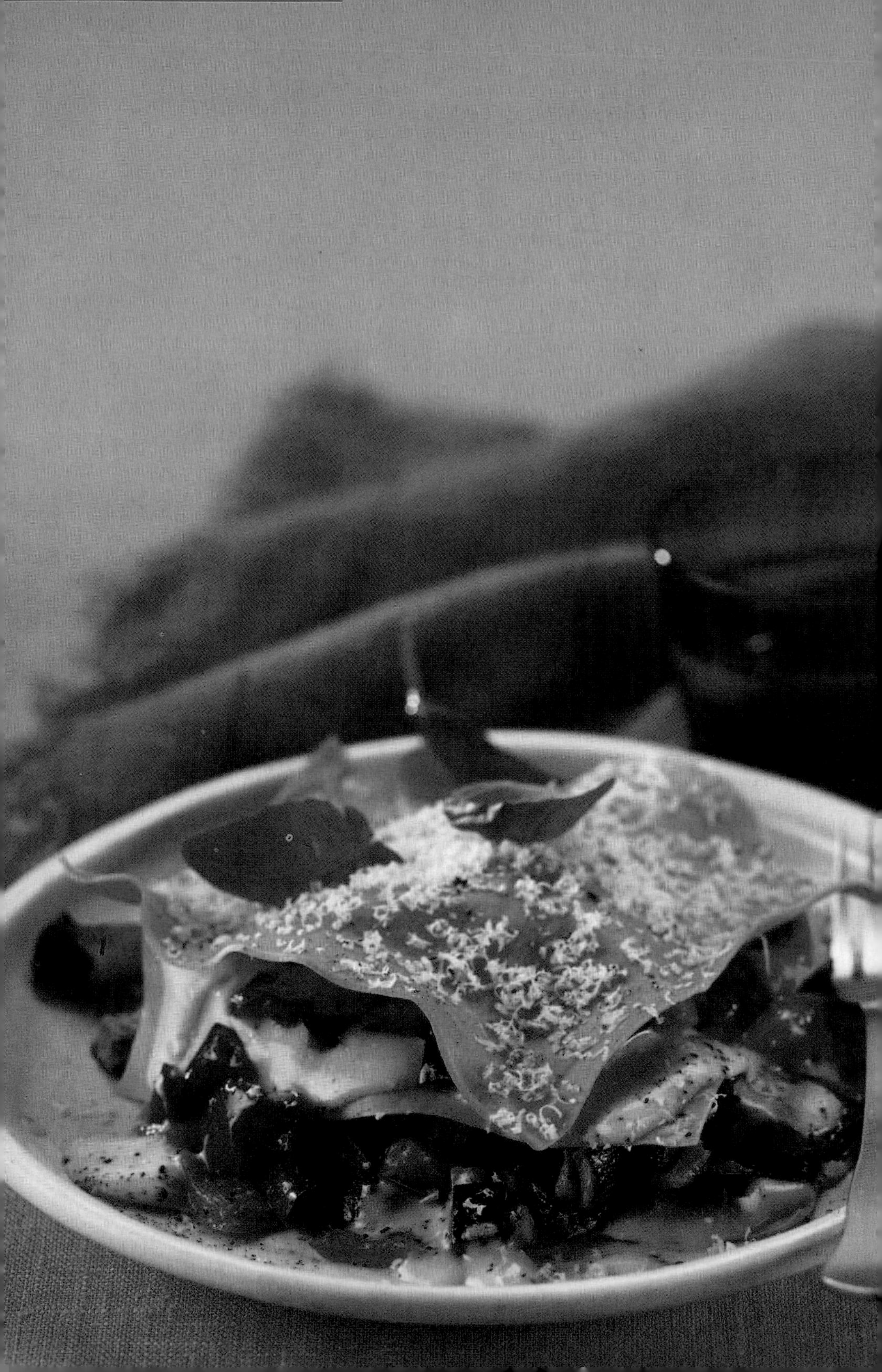

Open lasagne
with roasted vegetables

Serves 4
Ready in 40 minutes

1 aubergine (eggplant), about 250 g/9 oz

2 courgettes (zucchini)

1 red (bell) pepper and 1 yellow pepper, halved and seeded

2 garlic cloves, crushed

10 ml/2 tsp olive oil

Salt and freshly ground black pepper

For the sauce:

15 g/½ oz plain (all-purpose) flour

300 ml/½ pint/1¼ cups skimmed milk

1 bay leaf

A pinch of freshly grated nutmeg

To finish:

12 sheets of fresh lasagne

25 g/1 oz grated Parmesan cheese

Fresh basil leaves to garnish (optional)

1 Preheat the oven to 200°C/400°F/gas 6/fan oven 180°C. Cut the aubergine, courgettes and peppers into 1 cm/½ in cubes and place in a large non-stick roasting tin.

2 Mix together the garlic and oil and drizzle over the vegetables. Season with salt and pepper, then mix with your hands to coat the pieces. Roast for 20–25 minutes or until the vegetables are lightly browned and tender.

3 Meanwhile, to make the sauce, put the flour in a small saucepan and blend to a smooth paste with a little of the milk. Stir in the remaining milk, add the bay leaf, then bring to the boil, stirring all the time until smooth and thickened. Season with salt and the nutmeg.

4 Cook the lasagne sheets in boiling water according to the packet instructions, until *al dente* (tender but still firm to the bite). Drain and place in a single layer on a clean tea towel (dish cloth).

5 To assemble the dish, place a sheet of the cooked lasagne on each of four warm serving plates. Spoon a little of the sauce over, then spoon over some roasted vegetables. Repeat the layers, then top with a final sheet of lasagne. Sprinkle a little grated Parmesan and black pepper over each serving and garnish with a few basil leaves, if liked.

Index

aubergine (eggplant)
   Caribbean-style ratatouille 121
   grilled vegetable skewers 24
   open lasagne with roasted vegetables 125
   Turkish stuffed aubergines 114
avocado
   seafood salad 97

baby gherkins (cornichons)
   green herb dressing 94
balanced diet 5
banana
   wholemeal banana and walnut muffins 19
beansprouts
   Chinese-style pork 72
beef
   Mozzarella meatballs in rich tomato sauce 71
   mustard roast beef 67
   quick chilli beef 63
   seared beef with herb and horseradish mash 68
   spicy beef and broccoli 64
bell peppers see peppers
blue cheese
   roasted butternut squash with blue cheese and sage 109
bread
   chicken caesar salad 39
   hoisin turkey muffins 23
   lamb kebabs with cucumber and tomato salsa 79
   poached eggs and ham with watercress dressing 35
   roasted tomato and rocket bruschetta 36
   tasty tuna fishcakes 101
broccoli
   speedy vegetable stir-fry 118
   spicy beef and broccoli 64
butternut squash
   Caribbean-style ratatouille 121

cabbage
   herby polenta and mushrooms 113
Caribbean chicken with sweet potatoes 47
Caribbean-style ratatouille 121
carrots
   Chinese-style pork 72
   simple lamb hotpot 80
   speedy vegetable stir-fry 118
   spicy beef and broccoli 64
   turkey and tagliatelle sauté 59
   vegetarian shepherd's pie 110
cashew nuts
   Kashmiri chicken 43
Cheddar cheese
   nut loaf with tomato sauce 122
cheese
   fat content 8
   see also Cheddar cheese; Emmenthal cheese;
      Gorgonzola cheese; Mozzarella cheese; Parmesan
      cheese; ricotta cheese; soft cheese; Stilton cheese
chick peas (garbanzos)
   Moroccan chicken 51
chicken
   Caribbean chicken with sweet potatoes 47
   chicken caesar salad 39
   chicken salad wraps 44
   chicken skewers with couscous 48
   Kashmiri chicken 43
   Moroccan chicken 51
   warm chicken salad 52
chilli
   chilli and lime spatchcocked poussins 55
   chilli-baked plaice with hot onion relish 90
   hot and spicy pork 75
   quick chilli beef 63
   roasted butternut squash with blue cheese and sage 109
   seafood salad 97
   speedy vegetable stir-fry 118
Chinese-style pork 72

chocolate
   simple chocolate soufflés 19
cholesterol 6, 7
coconut milk
   Kashmiri chicken 43
   sweet potato and spinach 117
cod
   potato-topped cod with green herb dressing 94
cooking with low-fat methods 10-11, 59
cornichons, see baby gherkins
Cornish hens, see poussins, spatchcocked
courgettes (zucchini)
   Caribbean-style ratatouille 121
   chicken skewers with couscous 48
   mustard roast beef 67
   open lasagne with roasted vegetables 125
   roasted vegetable wraps 31
couscous
   chicken skewers with couscous 48
   griddled lamb and pepper skewers with minted tomato
      couscous 84
   Moroccan chicken 51
cream fat content 8
crème fraîche
   herb frittata with smoked salmon 93
   herby polenta and mushrooms 113
   seared beef with herb and horseradish mash 68
cucumber
   lamb kebabs with cucumber and tomato salsa 79

desserts
   quick and easy 18-19

egg noodles
   speedy vegetable stir-fry 118
   spicy beef and broccoli 64
eggs
   herb frittata with smoked salmon 93
   poached eggs and ham with watercress dressing 35
Emmenthal (Swiss) cheese
   herb frittata with smoked salmon 93
   herby polenta and mushrooms 113
essential fatty acids 6

fat
   and cooking oil 11
   easy ways to cut down 9-10
   food labels 7-8
   hydrogenated/trans 8
   low-fat cooking methods 10-11, 59
   monounsaturated 5
   polyunsaturated 6, 7
   recommended daily intake 6
   saturated 5, 7
feather-light pear pudding 18
Feta cheese
   Greek lamb casserole 83
fish
   fat content 8
   see also cod; plaice; salmon; seafood; tiger prawn;
      trout; tuna
five-spice trout and stir-fried vegetables 98
fluffy strawberry fool 19
food labels 7
fresh raspberry brulée 18

garbanzos, see chick peas
Gorgonzola cheese
   roasted butternut squash with blue cheese and sage 109
Greek lamb casserole 83
Greek yoghurt
   poached eggs and ham with watercress dressing 35
   ricotta tiramisu 19
green beans
   five-spice trout and stir-fried vegetables 98
green herb dressing 94

griddled lamb and pepper skewers with minted tomato couscous 84
griddled turkey goujons with tarragon and mustard dip 56
grilled vegetable skewers 24
guacamole
    roasted vegetable wraps 31

ham
    ham and cheese baked peppers 28
    poached eggs and ham with watercress dressing 35
herbs
    herb frittata with smoked salmon 93
    herby polenta and mushrooms 113
    potato-topped cod with green herb dressing 94
    roasted butternut squash with blue cheese and sage 109
    seared beef with herb and horseradish mash 68
hoisin sauce
hoisin turkey muffins 23
hot spiced tropical fruit kebabs 18
hot and spicy pork 75
houmous
    roasted vegetable wraps 31

Kashmiri chicken 43
kidney beans
    nutritional value 63
    quick chilli beef 63

lamb
    Greek lamb casserole 83
    griddled lamb and pepper skewers with minted tomato couscous 84
    lamb kebabs with cucumber and tomato salsa 79
    simple lamb hotpot 80
lasagne
    open lasagne with roasted vegetables 125
leeks
    leek, pea and Stilton soup 27
    nut loaf with tomato sauce 122
    roasted butternut squash with blue cheese and sage 109
lemon
    Moroccan chicken 51
    salmon teriyaki skewers with lemon rice 105
lentils
    nut loaf with tomato sauce 122
lettuce
    chicken caesar salad 39
    prawn noodle salad 32
lime
    chilli and lime spatchcocked poussins 55
    lamb kebabs with cucumber and tomato salsa 79
    lime dressing 52
    seafood salad 97

mangetout (snow peas)
    speedy vegetable stir-fry 118
mango
    hot spiced tropical fruit kebabs 18
meal plans and shopping lists 12–16
meat fat content 8
milk fat content 8
Moroccan chicken 51
Mozzarella cheese
    ham and cheese baked peppers 28
    Mozzarella meatballs in rich tomato sauce 71
mung bean noodles
    speedy vegetable stir-fry 118
mushrooms
    five-spice trout and stir-fried vegetables 98
    grilled vegetable skewers 24
    herby polenta and mushrooms 113
    hot and spicy pork 75
    nut loaf with tomato sauce 122
    quick chilli beef 63
mustard
    griddled turkey goujons with tarragon and mustard dip 56
    mustard roast beef 67
    warm chicken salad 52

noodles
    prawn noodle salad 32
    spicy beef and broccoli 64
    see also egg noodles; mung bean noodles; rice noodles

nuts
    loaf with tomato sauce 122
    see also cashew nuts
oils in cooking 11
olives
    Greek lamb casserole 83
omega-3/6 6

onions
    chilli-baked plaice with hot onion relish 90
    Mozzarella meatballs in rich tomato sauce 71
    mustard roast beef 67
    roasted vegetable wraps 31
    simple lamb hotpot 80
    spicy beef and broccoli 64
open lasagne with roasted vegetables 125
orange
    orange dressing 52
    seafood salad 97
    warm chicken salad 52

Parmesan cheese
    chicken caesar salad 39
    open lasagne with roasted vegetables 125
    roasted tomato and rocket bruschetta 36
    tasty tuna fishcakes 101
parsnip crips 27
pasta
    sweet potato and spinach pasta 117
    see also noodles; tagliatelle
pear
feather-light pear pudding 18
peas
    leek, pea and Stilton soup 27
    spicy pea dip 31
    vegetarian shepherd's pie 110
peppers (bell peppers)
    Caribbean chicken with sweet potatoes 47
    Caribbean-style ratatouille 121
    chicken salad wraps 44
    chicken skewers with couscous 48
    Chinese-style pork 72
    grilled vegetable skewers 24
    griddled lamb and pepper skewers with minted tomato couscous 84
    ham and cheese baked peppers 28
    open lasagne with roasted vegetables 125
    seafood paella 89
    roasted vegetable wraps 31
    seared beef with herb and horseradish mash 68
    speedy vegetable stir-fry 118
    turkey and tagliatelle sauté 59
pineapple
    hot spiced tropical fruit kebabs 18
plaice
    chilli-baked plaice with hot onion relish 90
planning a low-fat diet 7–9
    food labels 7
    your shopping basket 8
poached eggs and ham with watercress dressing 35
polenta
    as accompaniment 76
    herby polenta and mushrooms 113
pork
    Chinese-style pork 72
    hot and spicy pork 75
    Mozzarella meatballs in rich tomato sauce 71
potatoes
    Greek lamb casserole 83
    leek, pea and Stilton soup 27
    mustard roast beef 67
    potato-topped cod with green herb dressing 94
    seared beef with herb and horseradish mash 68
    simple lamb hotpot 80
    sweet potato and spinach 117
    tasty tuna fishcakes 101
poussins
    chilli and lime spatchcocked poussins 55
prawn noodle salad 32
pumpkin seeds
    nutritional value 52
    warm chicken salad 52

quick chilli beef 63
Quorn
  vegetarian shepherd's pie 110

raisins
  Turkish stuffed aubergines 114
raspberry
  fresh raspberry brulée 18
recipe notes 17
red wine
  venison sausages with red wine gravy 76
rice
  salmon teriyaki skewers with lemon rice 105
  seafood paella 89
rice noodles
  cooking instructions 75
  hot and spicy pork 75
  seafood salad 97
ricotta tiramisu 19
roasted butternut squash with blue cheese and sage 109
roasted tomato and rocket bruschetta 36
roasted vegetable wraps 31
rocket
  roasted tomato and rocket bruschetta 36

sage
  roasted butternut squash with blue cheese and sage 109
salmon
  herb frittata with smoked salmon 93
  salmon teriyaki skewers with lemon rice 105
  smoked salmon tagliatelle 102
seafood
seafood paella 89
seafood salad 97
seared beef with herb and horseradish mash 68
sesame seeds
  hoisin turkey muffins 23
  salmon teriyaki skewers with lemon rice 105
  speedy vegetable stir-fry 118
shallots
  grilled vegetable skewers 24
  Moroccan chicken 51
shrimp, see tiger prawns
simple chocolate soufflés 19
simple lamb hotpot 80
smoked salmon tagliatelle 102
snow peas, see mangetout
soft cheese
  smoked salmon tagliatelle 102
speedy vegetable stir-fry 118
spicy beef and broccoli 64
spinach
  Kashmiri chicken 43
  sweet potato and spinach 117
spring onions
  chicken salad wraps 44
  Chinese-style pork 72
  five-spice trout and stir-fried vegetables 98
  hoisin turkey muffins 23
  hot and spicy pork 75
  salmon teriyaki skewers with lemon rice 105
  warm chicken salad 52
squash
  roasted butternut squash with blue cheese and sage 109
squid
  seafood salad 97
Stilton cheese
  leek, pea and Stilton soup 27
  roasted butternut squash with blue cheese and sage 109
strawberry
  fluffy strawberry fool 19
sweet potatoes
  Caribbean chicken with sweet potatoes 47
  Caribbean-style ratatouille 121
  sweet potato and spinach 117
sweet treats 18-19
sweetcorn
  quick chilli beef 63

tagliatelle
  Mozzarella meatballs in rich tomato sauce 71

smoked salmon tagliatelle 102
turkey and tagliatelle sauté 59
see also noodles; pasta
tarragon
  chicken caesar salad 39
  griddled turkey goujons with tarragon and mustard dip 56
tasty tuna fishcakes 101
tiger prawns (shrimp)
  prawn noodle salad 32
  seafood salad 97
tomatoes
  Caribbean chicken with sweet potatoes 47
  Caribbean-style ratatouille 121
  chicken skewers with couscous 48
  Greek lamb casserole 83
  griddled lamb and pepper skewers with minted tomato couscous 84
  grilled vegetable skewers 24
  ham and cheese baked peppers 28
  how to skin 28
  lamb kebabs with cucumber and tomato salsa 79
  Mozzarella meatballs in rich tomato sauce 71
  nut loaf with tomato sauce 122
  quick chilli beef 63
  seafood paella 89
  roasted tomato and rocket bruschetta 36
  roasted vegetable wraps 31
  tomato pasta sauce 102
  tomato-pepper sauce 122
  turkey and tagliatelle sauté 59
  Turkish stuffed aubergines 114
  vegetarian shepherd's pie 110
  warm chicken salad 52
tortilla wraps
  chicken salad wraps 44
  roasted vegetable wraps 31
trout
  five-spice trout and stir-fried vegetables 98
tuna
tasty tuna fishcakes 101
turkey
  griddled turkey goujons with tarragon and mustard dip 56
  hoisin turkey muffins 23
  turkey and tagliatelle sauté 59
Turkish stuffed aubergines 114

vegetables
  Caribbean-style ratatouille 121
  grilled vegetable skewers 24
  open lasagne with roasted vegetables 125
  roasted vegetable wraps 31
  speedy vegetable stir-fry 118
  vegetarian shepherd's pie 110
vegetarian shepherd's pie 110
venison sausages with red wine gravy 76

walnut
  griddled lamb and pepper skewers with minted tomato couscous 84
  wholemeal banana and walnut muffins 19
warm chicken salad 52
water chestnuts
  speedy vegetable stir-fry 118
watercress
  poached eggs and ham with watercress dressing 35
wholemeal banana and walnut muffins 19

yoghurt
  chicken caesar salad 39
  fat content 8
  griddled turkey goujons with tarragon and mustard dip 56
  Kashmiri chicken 43
  lamb kebabs with cucumber and tomato salsa 79
  leek, pea and stilton soup 27
  see also Greek yoghurt

zucchini, see courgettes